design for tourism

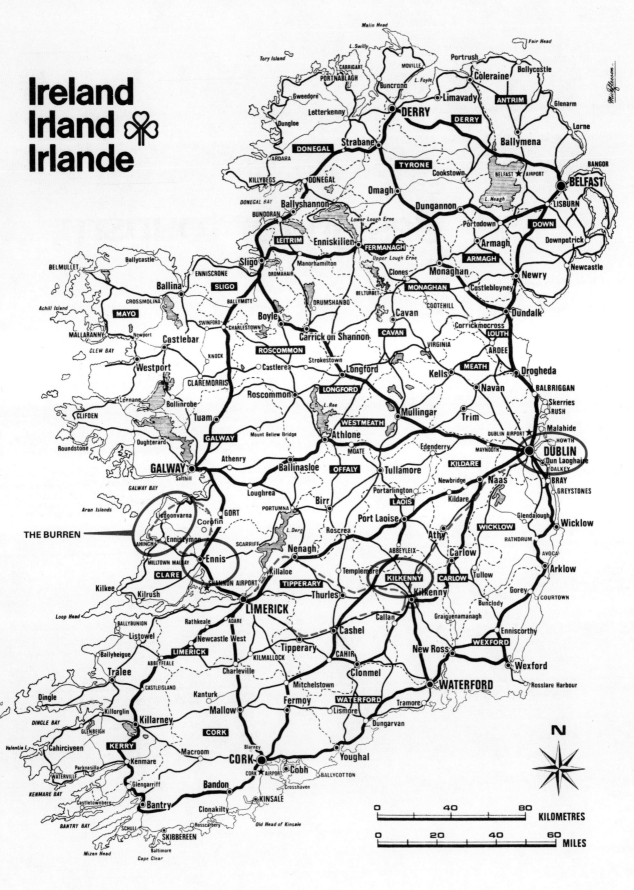

Ireland
Irland ✣
Irlande

THE BURREN

N

0	40	80

KILOMETRES

0	20	40	60

MILES

—————— Red indicates places mentioned in the report

– – – – – Blue indicates routes travelled

design for tourism

an ICSID inter design report

edited by Michael Gorman
Irish Tourist Board

Frank Height
Royal College of Art, London

Mary V. Mullin
Kilkenny Design Workshops

W. H. Walsh
Kilkenny Design Workshops

Published for ICSID by Pergamon Press
Oxford New York Toronto Sydney Paris Frankfurt

U.K.	Pergamon Press Ltd., Headington Hill Hall, Oxford OX3 0BW, England
U.S.A.	Pergamon Press Inc., Maxwell House, Fairview Park, Elmsford, New York 10523, U.S.A.
CANADA	Pergamon of Canada Ltd., 75 The East Mall, Toronto, Ontario, Canada
AUSTRALIA	Pergamon Press (Aust.) Pty. Ltd., 19a Boundary Street, Rushcutters Bay, N.S.W. 2011, Australia
FRANCE	Pergamon Press SARL, 24 rue des Ecoles, 75240 Paris, Cedex 05, France
WEST GERMANY	Pergamon Press GmbH, 6242 Kronberg-Taunus, Pferdstrasse 1, West Germany

First edition 1977

Library of Congress Cataloging in Publication Data

ICSID Interdesign Seminar, 2, Kilkenny, Ire., 1972.
Design for tourism.

1. Tourist trade—Congresses. I. Gorman, Michael.
II. International Council of Societies of Industrial Design. III. Title.
G155.A1I18 1972   338.4′7′91   76-58335
ISBN 0-08-021481-9

Arch. Folio

Printed in Great Britain by A. Wheaton & Co. Ltd., Exeter

Contents

Organising the Seminar

W. H. WALSH

We were happy to act as hosts to the second ICSID Interdesign Seminar, *Design for Tourism*. When the Kilkenny Design Workshops were founded in 1964 it was intended that we should, amongst other things, "pioneer new concepts in design".

Both for this reason and because Ireland has an important and growing tourist industry, the ICSID project of *Design for Tourism* had an immediate appeal for us. The implications which tourism can have for social and physical environment are a matter of national concern in Ireland, as they are in many countries. The proposal and recommendations of twenty professional designers coming together from different countries ought, we felt, to be of value not only to Ireland but to every country interested in tourism.

At the Congress at Ibiza in 1971 Kilkenny was decided on as the venue for the Design for Tourism Seminar. Background information and briefs were sent to the designers in advance of their arrival in May 1972. The project was divided into four groups:

    A. Holiday Accommodation
    B. Transport
    C. General Equipment
    D. Colour and Materials

The designers were formed into groups, more or less arbitrarily, to work on different sections, but as time went on a certain amount of regrouping came about naturally, as particular interests and professional affinities revealed themselves. It was clearly impracticable within the space of two weeks to carry out a comprehensive survey of the whole country. What was possible was a survey of a representative area, and County Clare was selected as the most appropriate. A week was devoted to field trips to allow members of the Seminar to obtain first-hand knowledge of the region. Their conclusions and recommendations were put on record during the week that followed. This was done, it should be emphasised, under considerable pressure.

Perhaps we were lucky in the calibre of the people who converged on Kilkenny from places as far removed from each other as Japan, Yugoslavia, Australia, and Finland. ICSID had screened the paper credentials of the applicants but, as in all such selections, an unpredictable element remained. Certainly we were lucky in the almost unbroken May sunshine which showed the Irish countryside at what one of the designers described as "its most heart-breakingly beautiful"

Few of the designers had any professional connection with the tourist industry. Yet within a remarkably short time the problems were identified and classified, and approaches to solutions defined. Instant teamwork evolved as if by magic. On the evidence of the two interdesign seminars held so far one must be impressed with the release of energy and the performance when a group of experienced professional designers comes together to engage on a project of social significance.

For the rest, it will be clear from reading the report that the participants have made a distinctive and important contribution to planning for tourism. At an early stage they rejected the idea of ready-made designs for specific situations as being inappropriate and quite possibly irrelevant, coming from those who had spent a mere two weeks in the country. It has been well said that "all introduced design is foreign and remains foreign until the people find a way of using it for themselves" So methods were devised to analyse needs and influences, to chart the interaction between guest and hosts, to illustrate the areas of common and separate use—in short to expose the problems and suggest solutions for a country which wants to keep its identity while propelled towards change by a rising tide of visitors.

We believe we can reasonably claim, therefore, that while Ireland happened to be the subject of this particular case study, the suggestions and conclusions in the report are relevant to all countries engaged in the tourist trade, which means a high proportion of the countries of the world.

Our co-hosts to the seminar were Bord Failte (the Irish Tourist Board) and Coras Trachtala (the Irish Export Board). We join with them in our thanks to the many people in Ireland and abroad, too numerous to mention by name, who helped in the organisation and the running of the seminar, and not least to the designers themselves who provided all the material for this report.

Special thanks are due to UNESCO whose financial assistance made this publication possible.

A Systematic Approach to a Design Problem

Introduction

Although the participants were divided into four groups, each one being given responsibility for one project brief, it became evident at the beginning of· the seminar that a number of the designers taking part felt that a general statement on a methodology of approach and the establishment of performance criteria should be prepared. This should be regarded as a statement on behalf of the whole seminar. The introductory statements that follow, therefore, can be regarded as a summary of many points made during discussions and policy meetings.

It was interesting to observe that this systematic concept was initiated in varying degrees by the groups in their approaches to their individual problems. Time, of course, did not allow the detailed application of such methodologies, but there is evidence of its usefulness in the partial applications which were made during the course of the seminar.

Analysis of the Task of the Seminar

Tourism is a social phenomenon arising from the development of industrialised societies.

It is a product of the following:

1. The wealth, earning capacity, and increasing amount of leisure time in developed countries.

2. The development of rapid mass transport systems.

3. The possibility of escape from familiar routines and surroundings, particularly from urban areas in industrial countries to countries promising unspoilt natural landscapes.

4. The possibility of contact with other life styles, exotic customs, language, and environments.

These factors are intensified by the commercial development of tourism by transport operators, hotel chains, and the authorities within potential host countries which have a direct interest in increasing the revenue from tourism.

This results in an increasingly large-scale need for tourist accommodation, which in turn intensifies the demand for the best sites in both towns and countryside and encourages a peripheral service network of facilities and amenities geared to the tourist, not to the residents, and frequently destructive of the essential qualities of the area.

The resulting imbalance creates a new kind of consumer society in undeveloped areas—a tourist consumer society. A conflict therefore arises between the needs and wishes of tourists who live and work in an industrial society and the economic benefits that tourism can bring to a developing society. This conflict can be expressed in the form of a diagram.

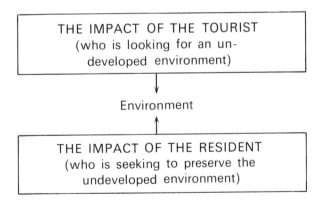

Informative and Educative

The members of the seminar generally support the view expressed by An Foras Forbartha (the National Institute for Physical Planning and Construction Research) that public education must take place about the major conflicts which can arise between the demands of tourists, on the one hand, and local residents, on the other. The understanding of this problem is fundamental to an approach to design for tourism.

Tourism should be seen as a continuing social and educational process. Guide-books, brochures, and other forms of tourist information are devices which condition the tourist to "see" the country through the "eyes" of promotional material, but they should be viewed as components of a wider system of communication. Information for children, teenagers, and adult travellers should be co-ordinated with planning for national and regional development and with the objectives of the Tourist Board.

Policies and action for developing and catering for tourism should preferably be included within the existing planning framework rather than superimposed on it from outside.

An Foras Forbartha and Bord Failte state among their objectives that "areas of High National Amenity" should be protected from indiscriminate development by either tourist or local resident activities or wants, and refer to "environmental objectives such as conservation and development control". This suggests that one of the design objectives of the seminar should be in support of this. Apart from tourist or local resident "wants" there exists the need to consider design in the socio-physical sense rather than as a purely visual technique. Resource allocation and management are not products for tourism to be indiscriminately distributed throughout the countryside—"Not a good design" label everywhere but rather a "design not necessary" label.

What is Tourism?

Touring, which is the business if not the essence of tourism, means moving from one environment to another. Tourism is the opportunity and ability to see how local people live and to share some part of that life with them.

These general observations are applicable to tourism in most countries. They provide a social and economic context within which we can examine the particular problems of tourism whether in Ireland or elsewhere.

It is obvious that problems of accommodation, transport equipment, and materials cannot be considered in isolation unrelated to the following factors:

1. The appreciation and understanding of the natural (existing) environment.

2. The need and capacity for economic development.

3. The political forces controlling economic factors.

There are two broad categories of resources:

(a) Those which *attract* the visitor or the resident.

Touring	Caravanning Motor Horse
	Coach
	Car
	Cycle
Activity	Hunting (fox, stag, deer, etc.)
	Shooting (game, birds, fowl, etc.)
	Fishing (coarse, game, sea)
	Riding (pony trekking)
	Boating (canoeing, yachting)
	Water sports (skin-diving, skiing)
	Spectator sports (racing, show jumping)
	Organised sports and activities
	Walking and hiking, etc.
Manmade	Ethnic and religious (historical and educational)
	Great houses and gardens
	Architecture and archaeology
	Gallery and museum, etc.
Physical	Landscape (mountain, river and lake)
	Seascape

(b) Those which *serve* him.

Facilities	Food and entertainment
Accommodation	Hotels, farmhouses, guesthouses, cottages, summer houses, condominiums, caravan sites, hostels, schools, and camps

Utilities

Communications and transport

Evaluation

The natural environment complete with its manmade activities is the fundamental resource for tourist needs.

For tourist satisfaction to prevail, tourism must remain, or appear to remain, secondary to some primary activity or resource. In other words, the environment does not exist for the sake of the tourist.

The Tourists' Need

Tourists wish to see Ireland as it is:
—Picturesque
—Historical
—Romantic
—Landscape
—Agrarian/rural living condition

The Need of The Irish People

Irish people wish to see Ireland developed, to feel the sense of going somewhere and not to be considered inhabitants of a tourist museum.

Yet tourism is an industry.

It is obviously impossible to study the effects of tourism without also studying what the IRISH wish to become.

Analysis

As part of the preliminary investigatory examination of the Seminar theme a small group undertook a study of method and criteria applicable for the consideration of tourism. Diagrams were developed to show the intricate system of interrelationships which must be taken into account. They were drawn up to enable a general and common approach to be made to the problems of tourism anywhere in the world. The diagrams reproduced on the end papers of this volume were subsequently revised by Daryl Jackson, a member of the group, for publication,[1] and it is in the revised version that they are shown.

Design Australia, February/March, 1973.

Figure 1.   The key interaction network sets out national aims and goals in relation to tourism. It is subdivided into various blocks of information and shows the relation between them and the bodies or organisations who are responsible for them. The tourist authority should take all this information into account.

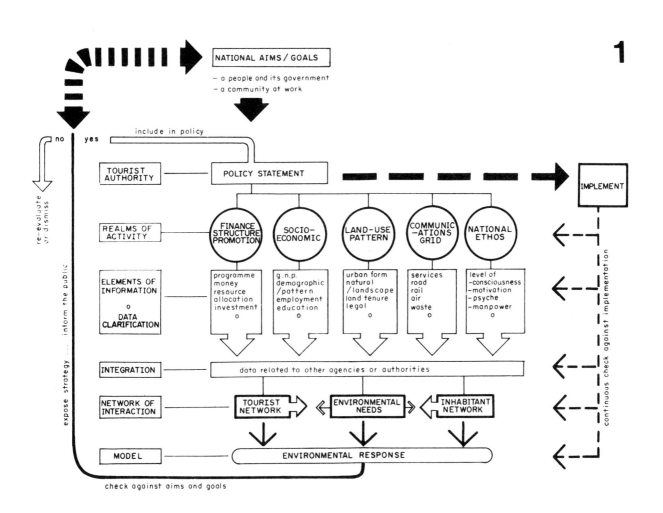

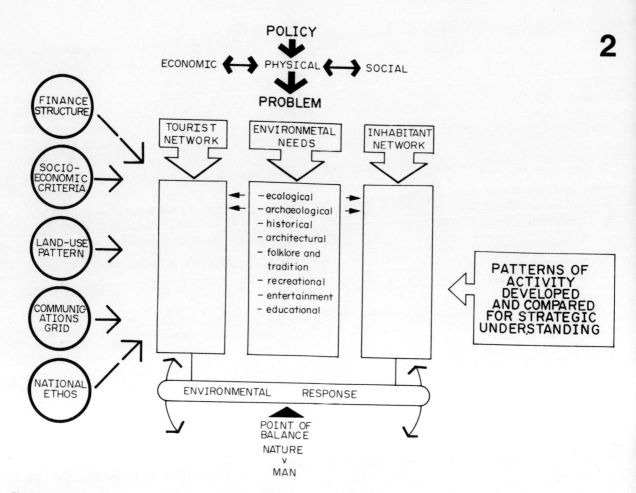

Figure 2. The interaction between the tourist, the environment, and the residents; the people who live in the country and who have created and used the environment. This is a network of what tourists do and what residents do. One of the objectives should be to achieve a balance between the economic and social position and the environmental needs of the country.

Figure 3. The interactions of international phenomena. This analyses the tourists: their activities, where they are from, type, age, their requirements and interests, methods of travel, etc. It is possible to make up an image of the tourist and his effect on the residents, and of their effect upon him. All this will help to direct policy and decide what action should be taken and what the process is that determines it.

Figure 4. A description of the design process, illustrating the way in which a planning team relates to a planning committee as tourist authority.

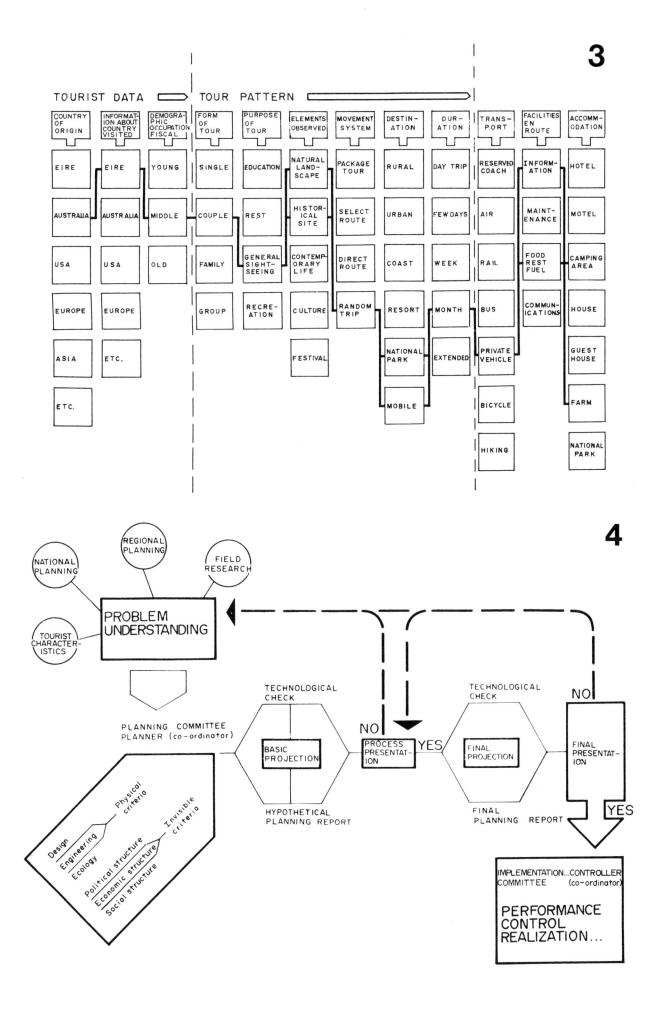

3

TOURIST DATA			TOUR PATTERN								
COUNTRY OF ORIGIN	INFORMATION ABOUT COUNTRY VISITED	DEMOGRAPHIC OCCUPATION FISCAL	FORM OF TOUR	PURPOSE OF TOUR	ELEMENTS OBSERVED	MOVEMENT SYSTEM	DESTINATION	DURATION	TRANSPORT	FACILITIES EN ROUTE	ACCOMMODATION
EIRE	EIRE	YOUNG	SINGLE	EDUCATION	NATURAL LANDSCAPE	PACKAGE TOUR	RURAL	DAY TRIP	RESERVED COACH	INFORMATION	HOTEL
AUSTRALIA	AUSTRALIA	MIDDLE	COUPLE	REST	HISTORICAL SITE	SELECT ROUTE	URBAN	FEW DAYS	AIR	MAINTENANCE	MOTEL
USA	USA	OLD	FAMILY	GENERAL SIGHTSEEING	CONTEMPORARY LIFE	DIRECT ROUTE	COAST	WEEK	RAIL	FOOD REST FUEL	CAMPING AREA
EUROPE	EUROPE		GROUP	RECREATION	CULTURE	RANDOM TRIP	RESORT	MONTH	BUS	COMMUNICATIONS	HOUSE
ASIA	ETC.				FESTIVAL		NATIONAL PARK	EXTENDED	PRIVATE VEHICLE		GUEST HOUSE
ETC.							MOBILE		BICYCLE		FARM
									HIKING		NATIONAL PARK

4

PROBLEM UNDERSTANDING

NATIONAL PLANNING
REGIONAL PLANNING
FIELD RESEARCH
TOURIST CHARACTERISTICS

PLANNING COMMITTEE
PLANNER (co-ordinator)

Design
Engineering
Ecology
Physical criteria
Political structure
Economic structure
Social structure
Invisible criteria

TECHNOLOGICAL CHECK
BASIC PROJECTION
HYPOTHETICAL PLANNING REPORT

NO
PROCESS PRESENTATION
YES

TECHNOLOGICAL CHECK
FINAL PROJECTION
FINAL PLANNING REPORT

NO
FINAL PRESENTATION
YES

IMPLEMENTATION...CONTROLLER COMMITTEE (co-ordinator)

PERFORMANCE CONTROL REALIZATION...

Group A
Holiday Accommodation

This group was concerned with the design of holiday accommodation. Members stayed, as part of a preliminary field trip, in the following:

(a) a grade A hotel in Dublin;
(b) a grade A hotel in a country town;
(c) a luxury motor hotel;
(d) an international style motor hotel;
(e) a farmhouse;
(f) a rented cottage.

This research provided a wide experience of the present situation in Ireland.

The Brief

A standard type of modern hotel has appeared throughout the world, often erected indiscriminately in areas of special character or natural beauty and destructive of the quality of the environment.

In Ireland there are farmhouses and similar buildings, indigenous to the countryside, some of which have been converted to provide holiday accommodation. Participants were asked to study this development with the object of enlarging its scope and in particular to make proposals for:

(a) conversion and extension of existing buildings;
(b) the equipping, furnishing, and interior decoration of such buildings.

The proposals were to be framed so as to preserve or enhance the quality of the area and at the same time provide accommodation suitable to the needs of modern tourists.

It was suggested that Group A's investigation and proposals might fall into the following three parts, each of which might attempt to produce ideas relevant to the needs of holidays in Ireland:

1. Evaluation of and recommendations on the existing situation observed during the field trips, e.g. what aspects of the present accommodation, furnishing, and equipment are acceptable and capable of development and which should be altered?
2. Design proposals for the new development or conversion of existing buildings. These should aim at general rather than special cases.
3. Design proposals for the equipment and furnishing of holiday accommodation.

The Group saw its task as evaluation of the existing situation as observed during the field trips and putting forward recommendations based on that evaluation (which aspects of the present accommodation, furnishing, and equipment are acceptable and capable of development, and which should be altered).

It undertook to produce two kinds of design proposals:

1. For the development of new buildings or the conversion of existing buildings.
2. For the equipment and furnishing of holiday accommodation.

It was felt that these should aim at general rather than special cases.

Group Results

An initial commentary was made on large international hotels and motor hotels which pose one of the most obvious and dramatic threats to the countryside. In particular the problem of siting, not only in areas of natural beauty but in relation to small towns where such hotels provide powerful competition as a centre of life and employment, was examined.

Detailed studies were made into the conversion and extension of existing indigenous buildings such as farmhouses and into the planning and integration of new buildings in the landscape and in small farm and village clusters.

Particular studies were made of condominium

units which may become an increasingly used method of providing relatively high density holiday accommodation in a controlled and compact way and of rented cottages which relate not only to the landscape but to the vernacular of the Irish cottage.

Figure A1. The checklist is for use by different types of accommodation operators, enabling them to assess their strengths and weaknesses. It demonstrates the wide range of factors requiring consideration. The checklist can be used to provide an inventory of accommodation providing various types of activity, facilities, or according to the natural resources.

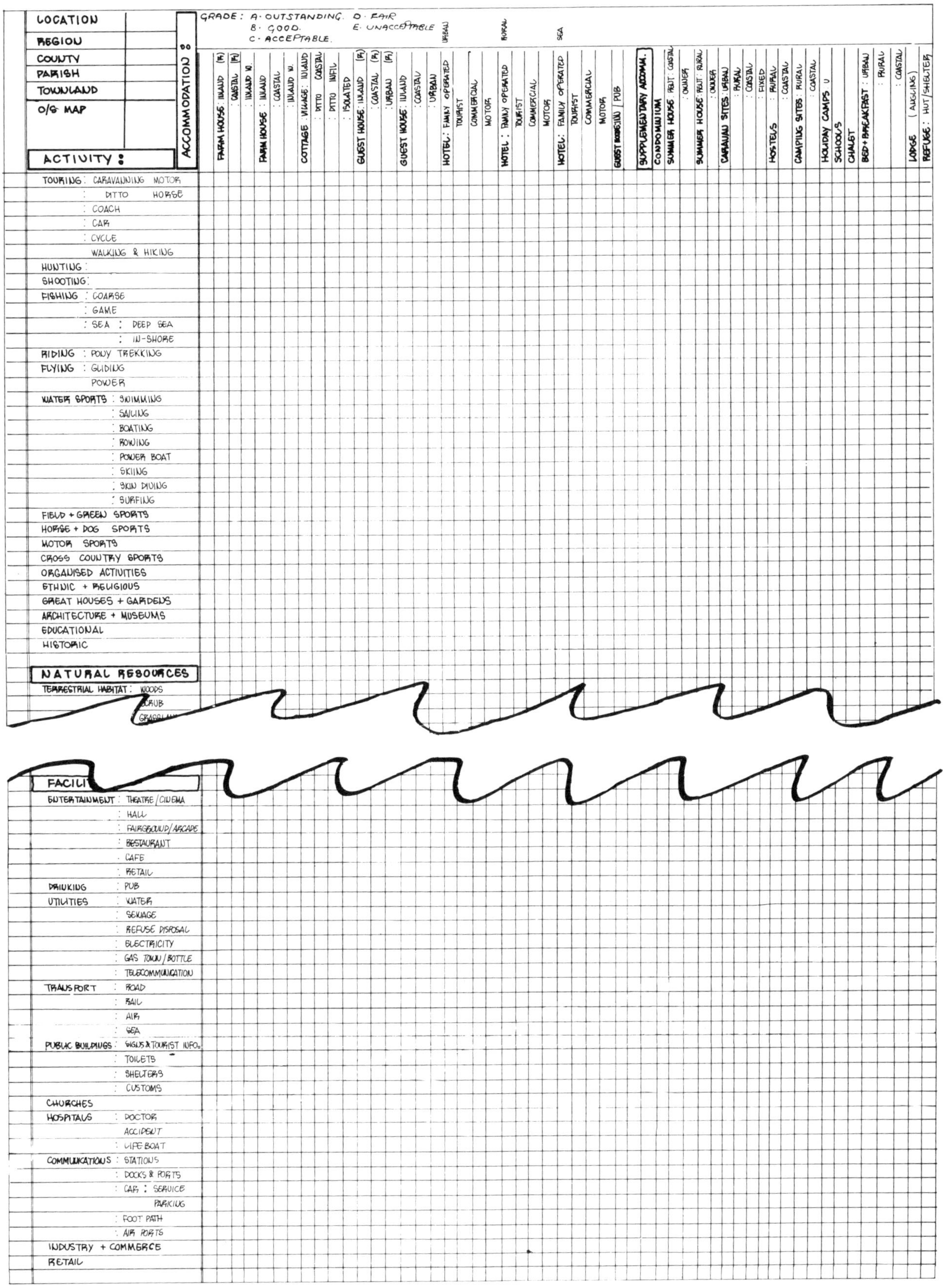

LOCATION
REGION
COUNTY
PARISH
TOWNLAND
O/S MAP

ACCOMMODATION

GRADE: A · OUTSTANDING. D · FAIR
B · GOOD. E · UNACCEPTABLE
C · ACCEPTABLE.

FARM HOUSE: INLAND (PR) / COASTAL (PR)
FARM HOUSE: INLAND VI / COASTAL / INLAND VI / COASTAL VI
COTTAGE: VILLAGE INLAND / DITTO COASTAL / DITTO INFILL / ISOLATED
GUEST HOUSE: INLAND (PR) / COASTAL (PR) / INLAND / COASTAL / URBAN
GUEST HOUSE: INLAND / COASTAL / URBAN
HOTEL: FAMILY OPERATED / TOURIST / COMMERCIAL / MOTOR
HOTEL: FAMILY OPERATED / TOURIST / COMMERCIAL / MOTOR
HOTEL: FAMILY OPERATED / TOURIST / COMMERCIAL / MOTOR
GUEST ROOM (IN) / PUB
SUPPLEMENTARY ACCOMM.
CONDOMINIUM
SUMMER HOUSE FRUIT COASTAL / OUVRIER
SUMMER HOUSE FRUIT RURAL / OUVRIER
CARAVAN SITES: URBAN / RURAL / COASTAL / FIXED
HOSTELS: RURAL / COASTAL
CAMPING SITES: RURAL / COASTAL
HOLIDAY CAMPS U
SCHOOLS
CHALET
BED + BREAKFAST: URBAN / RURAL / COASTAL
LODGE (AUXILING)
REFUGE: HUT/SHELTER

URBAN / RURAL / SEA

ACTIVITY :

TOURING : CARAVANING MOTOR
: DITTO HORSE
: COACH
: CAR
: CYCLE
: WALKING & HIKING
HUNTING :
SHOOTING :
FISHING : COARSE
: GAME
: SEA : DEEP SEA
: IN-SHORE
RIDING : PONY TREKKING
FLYING : GLIDING
POWER
WATER SPORTS : SWIMMING
: SAILING
: BOATING
: ROWING
: POWER BOAT
: SKIING
: SKIN DIVING
: SURFING
FIELD + GREEN SPORTS
HORSE + DOG SPORTS
MOTOR SPORTS
CROSS COUNTRY SPORTS
ORGANISED ACTIVITIES
ETHNIC + RELIGIOUS
GREAT HOUSES + GARDENS
ARCHITECTURE + MUSEUMS
EDUCATIONAL
HISTORIC

NATURAL RESOURCES
TERRESTRIAL HABITAT : WOODS
SCRUB
GRASSLAND

FACILI...
ENTERTAINMENT : THEATRE / CINEMA
: HALL
: FAIRGROUND / ARCADE
: RESTAURANT
: CAFE
: RETAIL
DRINKING : PUB
UTILITIES : WATER
: SEWAGE
: REFUSE DISPOSAL
: ELECTRICITY
: GAS TOWN / BOTTLE
: TELECOMMUNICATION
TRANSPORT : ROAD
: RAIL
: AIR
: SEA
PUBLIC BUILDINGS : SIGNS & TOURIST INFO.
: TOILETS
: SHELTERS
: CUSTOMS
CHURCHES
HOSPITALS : DOCTOR
: ACCIDENT
: LIFE BOAT
COMMUNICATIONS : STATIONS
: DOCKS & PORTS
: CAR : SERVICE
: PARKING
: FOOT PATH
: AIR PORTS
INDUSTRY + COMMERCE
RETAIL

The Impact of New Development

The development of new accommodation, instead of improving existing buildings, facilities, and amenities, has resulted in the deterioration of existing hotels.

When, as is common, a new hotel is built on the outskirts of a town or village the tendency is for the social centre to move with it to the detriment of the life of the town or village.

In villages and towns where there are run-down structures such as mills, castles, and warehouses, the owners, developers, and tourist authorities should investigate and, wherever possible, recommend the conversion of these old buildings before undertaking new work. The conversion and improvement of existing structures results in physical and social gains.

Interior treatment should relate to the style and type of building and the materials used.

Furnishing and equipment should be of local manufacture whenever possible and of good quality. Emphasis should be placed on the use of natural materials and landscape colours. The colours of the Irish landscape range through soft brown, yellow/orange/ochre, grey/green/sea green, and act as a foil to the use of a wide variety of intense and rich colours.

These are only guidelines. The precise manner in which individual owners use materials and colours will emphasise the distinctive character of the local scene. The Group considered this important, as ill-considered, deliberate attempts to design for "Irishness" tend to caricature rather than to enhance local characteristics.

The "International" Type Hotel

A standard type of modern hotel has appeared throughout the world, often erected indiscriminately in areas of special character and great natural beauty, and destructive of the quality of the environment.

In this statement "a standard type of modern hotel" is understood to describe an hotel catering to a wide variety of tourist needs, such as sleeping, eating, entertainment, shopping, recreation, sports, and conventions, though this last is not always included, and having a large number (300–400) of bedrooms. The reasons for the appearance of the standard type of modern hotel results from the economic advantages of providing many and varied facilities for a large number of tourists in an attractive environment of "great natural beauty". *The location is the prime attraction.*

This multi-purpose leisure-type complex has little or no architectural precedent (except in nineteenth-century continental spas such as Marienbad), and most of the current architectural solutions are dictated by:

1. Pressures to build cheaply and quickly buildings which have to pay their way and which are in use often for a short season only.

2. Environmental factors such as the nature of the site, i.e. remote location, absence of existing services, climate.

3. The fact that there is often no existing man-made environment to which to relate the new structures.

These hotels are rarely beautiful except in the eyes of the owner and perhaps of the tourist who, in a holiday mood, with creature comforts well catered for, lives in the hotel for only a short time. He is not critical of his environment and may not even be aware of the eventual destruction of his pleasant holiday surroundings.

The siting of this type of hotel and other types of new development outside small towns and cities, and removed from the social centre, has a detrimental effect on social activity in the town itself.

The Group felt that it would be of greater benefit to a town from a social and planning point of view (no derelict sites or empty boarded-up buildings), and to the tourist industry to reactivate existing structures and plants than to build outside the town new hotels, however comfortable, which ignored the character of their surroundings. When making this recommendation it was acknowledged that the reactivation of existing plant would be expensive, less productive of revenue, and require greater effort and co-operation between planners and developers than exists at present. But it was also felt that the planning authorities, local and national, have an overriding responsibility in this matter.

Two existing, well-established town hotels were visited by the Group in Wexford and in Ennis, whose facilities had been extended to meet modern requirements by providing extra amenities, and whose owners and architects have made successful efforts to enlarge these hotels and to enhance the character of the buildings and location. This type of hotel development is a trend which should be encouraged.

That Ireland has so far been spared much poor and destructive development was felt to be due to:

1. Efforts of Foras Forbartha and related bodies such as An Taisce (the National Trust for Ireland).

2. Local and national planning authorities' vigilance.

Figure A2. This type of hotel could generally be developed in small towns and villages. The form of the buildings shown indicates how they might be integrated into a holiday village cluster.

3. The efforts of Bord Failte in making an effort to guide the location and design of the various types of tourist plant.

4. The people themselves being aware of and protective of their natural resources.

5. The fact that Ireland's full potential for tourism has not yet been realised. When this potential comes to be recognised, dangers to areas of great natural beauty can be avoided if the guidelines laid down by the Coastal Survey are adopted and implemented by planning authorities. Warning would be taken from the destruction done to areas of attraction and good environment everywhere.

2 *Building*
Existing buildings
New buildings
Direct labour
Contract
Traditional style
Modern

3 *Operation*
Advertising and marketing
Management professional
Service
Maintenance
Host
Principal supervisor
   (regular supervision)
Cook
Assistant cook
Trained kitchen helps

Performance Criteria for Family-operated Hotel

This checklist was evolved for use by family hotel owners. It indicates the wide range of considerations which must be taken into account and evaluated when changes are being made.

Resources

1 *Financial*
Private
Grants
Loans
Shares

Environmental framework

1 *External*
Siting and landscape
Appearance
Location
Aspect
Prospect
Access

2 *Internal*
Eating and drinking
Cooking
Sleeping and bathing
Recreation
Decoration

Recreational

Touring: car
Hunting and shooting
Fishing
Riding
Water sports
Field and green sports
Cross-country sports

Social frame

Suitable for
Family
Married couple with young children
Individuals

Accommodation
Reception and entrance
Dining space—minimum to accommodate 30
persons—200 sq. ft.
Kitchen and preparation (Food Hygiene
Regulations 1950)
Service
Dispence bar
Lounge: Communal area
Wet day and TV area
Bedrooms: at least 10 units
Single: 80 sq. ft. (can be less)
Double: 130 sq. ft. (can be less)
At least all double rooms to have private
bathroom (but recommended for all rooms)
Furniture and fittings of good quality
(Bathroom and toilet: to unserviced rooms)
Cloakrooms
Public toilets

Services
Heating (minimum 65°) through the premises
Hot and cold water
Fresh water to all bedrooms
Telephone on the premises
Sewage and waste services

FARMHOUSE ACCOMMODATION —A CASE STUDY

This study was concerned with ways of increasing the guest capacity of a farmhouse so as to increase earnings from tourism in a way which would maintain and enhance the quality of life of the farm family.

The factors considered were the physical and human resources, the available finance, the estimated return on investment, and the environmental and recreational factors.

Lahardan Farmhouse, Crusheen, Co. Clare

Lahardan is a working farm where the owners take in guests and need to enlarge the existing accommodation for their own and tourist needs. Figure 2 (Jackson) illustrated the performance criteria for every type of tourist accommodation and assessed the programme of development required to meet the needs of tourists and the owner/manager without impairing the quality of character of the accommodation itself. This method was applied by the Group to Lahardan.

The following possible solutions were considered:

1. To increase guest capacity within the existing structure.

2. To build on to the existing building.

3. To adapt the existing farm outbuildings, i.e. gate-lodge, stable.

4. To build a self-contained letting unit on the farm.

5. To maintain the buildings and facilities as they are at present.

The Group agreed that the following development programme would meet the need for more accommodation and at the same time improving the quality of the buildings.

Phase 1. To put a roof on the flat-roofed extension.

Phase 2. To adapt the stables to form a unit for renting. This unit provides self-contained accommodation for 6–8 people.

Phase 3. To build a new self-contained unit for renting near the farmyard and located so as not to interfere with the existing layout of the farmyard and the house.

The design of the cottage pays attention to the character and structure of the farm buildings, the informal layout of the yard, and the wooded nature of the surroundings.

Figure A3. This figure demonstrates how major development could increase tourist capacity of Lahardan Farmhouse substantially in keeping with the general character of its setting and with minimum destructive impact.

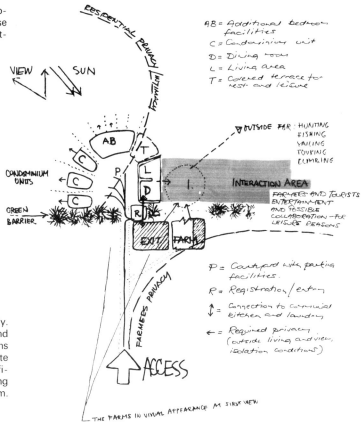

VIEW   SUN

RESIDENTIAL PRIVACY/ISOLATION

AB = Additional bedroom facilities
C = Condominium unit
D = Dining room
L = Living area
T = Covered terrace for rest and leisure

OUTSIDE FAR: HUNTING
FISHING
SAILING
TOURING
CLIMBING

INTERACTION AREA

FARMERS AND TOURISTS ENTERTAINMENT AND POSSIBLE COLLABORATION - FOR LEISURE REASONS

CONDOMINIUM UNITS

GREEN BARRIER

EXIT FARM

P = Courtyard with parking facilities.
R = Registration/entry
↕ = Connection to communal kitchen and laundry
← = Required privacy (outside living and view, isolation conditions)

FARMERS PRIVACY

ACCESS

THE FARMS IN VISUAL APPEARANCE AT FIRST VIEW

Figure A4. Farmhouse accommodation varies greatly. Lahardan, not far from Ennis, Co. Clare, in the west of Ireland was selected for this study. It presented many of the problems to be faced in extending an old farm building to accommodate additional tourists. It was accepted that extensions and modifications should be in harmony and character with the existing structure and setting and if possible should enhance them.

1. The approach to Lahardan Farm.
A, Attractive impression created by approach is destroyed when visitor arrives at this point. B, Covered way out of character with main structure. Wrong use of materials. C, Flat roof out of character with existing main structure. D, Do-it-yourself building techniques—unsatisfactory results. E, Sub-standard family accommodation built to enable more guests to be housed in main structure.

2. Approach to house showing well-cared for appearance. An inviting place to stay.
At this point the haphazard extension policy is not apparent.
3. Out of "site" out of mind. Rear of house showing haphazard approach to accommodation extensions.
4. Simple inexpensive furnishings in character with building of type of accommodation being offered.

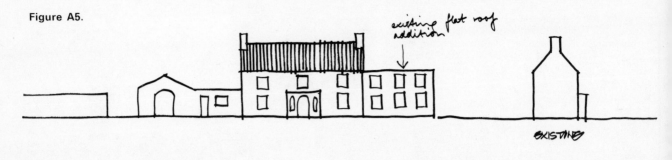

existing flat roof
addition

EXISTING

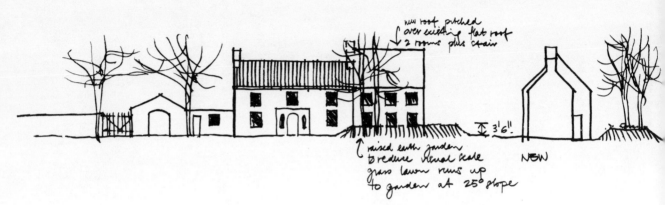

new roof pitched
over existing flat roof
2 rooms plus stair

3'6"

raised earth garden
to reduce visual scale
grass lawn runs up
to garden at 25° slope

NEW

Figure A6. Existing building with pitched roof added to existing flat-roofed extension.

PLACE PITCHED ROOF
ON EXISTING ADDITION

LANDSCAPE TREES
AND EARTH BANK TO
REDUCE IMPACT OF
EXISTING OLD AND NEW

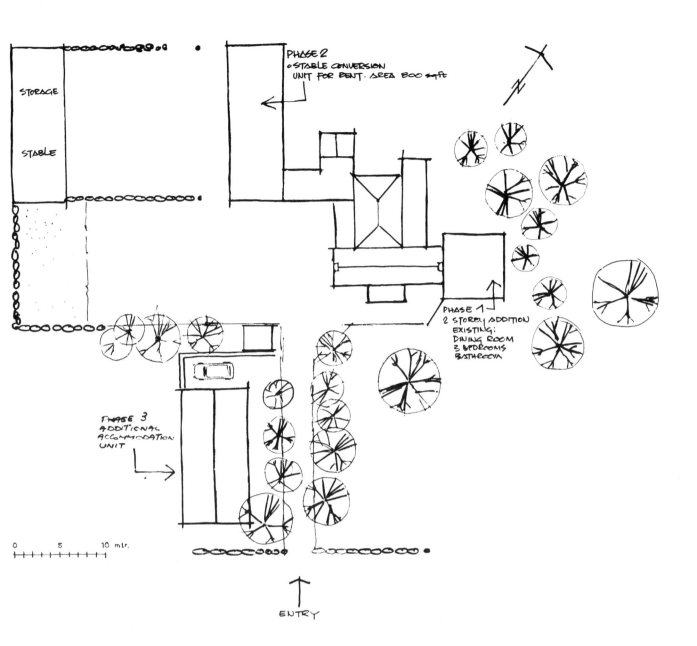

STORAGE

STABLE

PHASE 2
o STABLE CONVERSION
UNIT FOR RENT. AREA 800 sqft

N

PHASE 1
2 STOREY ADDITION
EXISTING:
DINING ROOM
3 BEDROOMS
BATHROOM

PHASE 3
ADDITIONAL
ACCOMMODATION
UNIT

0 5 10 mtr.

ENTRY

Figure A7.   Planned development.

Figure A8.   Ground floor.

Figure A9.   First floor.

Figure A10.   Alternative use of stables and outbuildings.

Figure A11.   Additional accommodation unit.

Figure A12.   Additional accommodation in stable unit conversion.

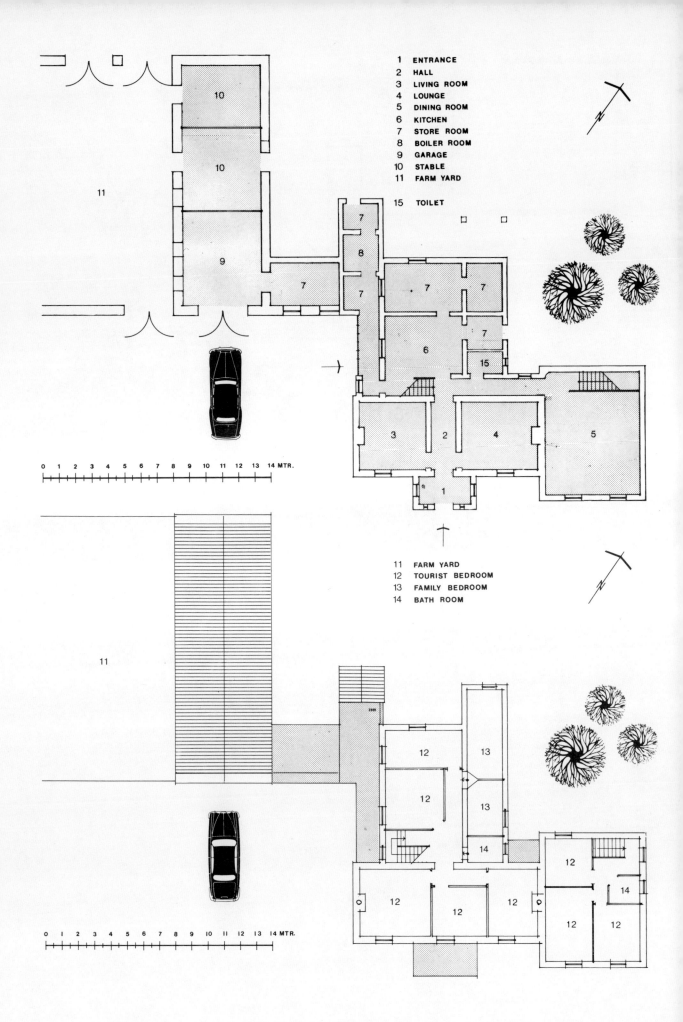

1 ENTRANCE
2 HALL
3 LIVING ROOM
4 LOUNGE
5 DINING ROOM
6 KITCHEN
7 STORE ROOM
8 BOILER ROOM
9 GARAGE
10 STABLE
11 FARM YARD

15 TOILET

0 1 2 3 4 5 6 7 8 9 10 11 12 13 14 MTR.

11 FARM YARD
12 TOURIST BEDROOM
13 FAMILY BEDROOM
14 BATH ROOM

0 1 2 3 4 5 6 7 8 9 10 11 12 13 14 MTR.

22

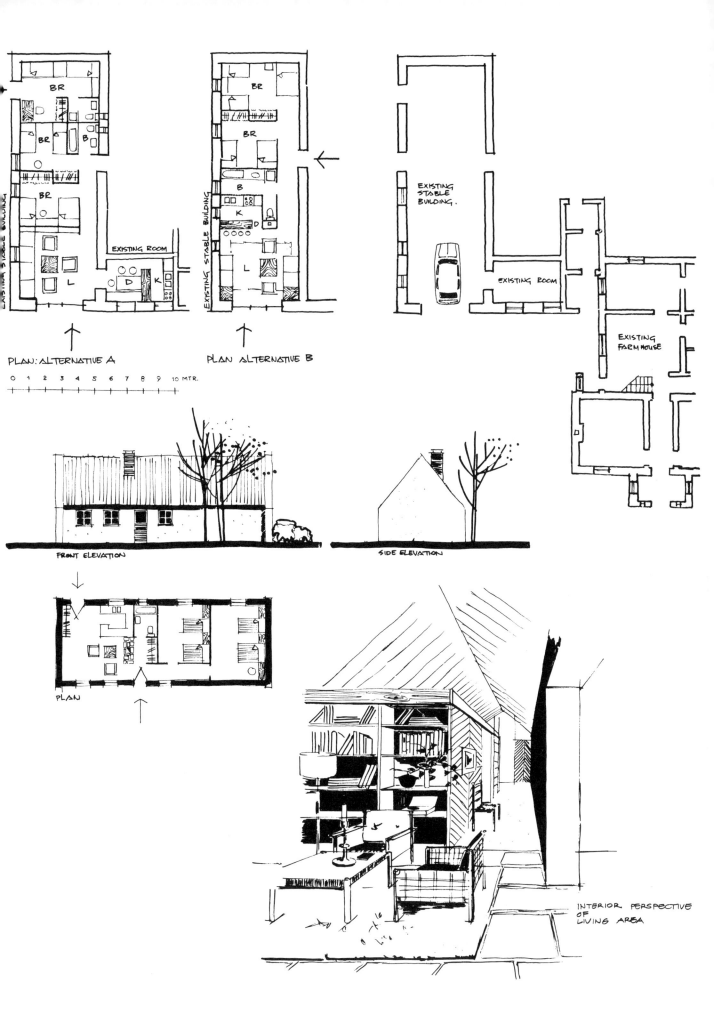

BR

BR B

BR

L D K

EXISTING ROOM

EXISTING STABLE BUILDING

PLAN: ALTERNATIVE A

BR

BR

B

K D

L

EXISTING STABLE BUILDING

PLAN ALTERNATIVE B

0 1 2 3 4 5 6 7 8 9 10 MTR.

EXISTING STABLE BUILDING.

EXISTING ROOM

EXISTING FARM HOUSE

FRONT ELEVATION

SIDE ELEVATION

PLAN

INTERIOR PERSPECTIVE OF LIVING AREA

23

CONDOMINIUMS

A second possibility was the design of condominium units.

A form of condominium—that of partnership between landowner and the user of accommodation—was studied by Group A, its essential feature being that of a controlled co-operative development.

The Condominium

One proposal shows a group of vacation houses constructed in a vacant field adjacent to an existing farmhouse (Fig. A13). It is envisaged that the farmer could lease the land to each condominium owner. This would augment the farm income.

The condominium (or company of neighbouring vacation-house owners) would take the form of a legal partnership which included the landowner. This would maintain a harmony of design between one house and another. Flexibility, if this were required, could be achieved by varying the size of the houses.

Individual owners could arrange to let their houses to tourists for vacations if they so desired, with the farmer providing some management services for which he would be paid. Such a scheme would suit second home owners from the urban areas of Ireland or from abroad.

Figure A13. Condominium houses added to existent farms.

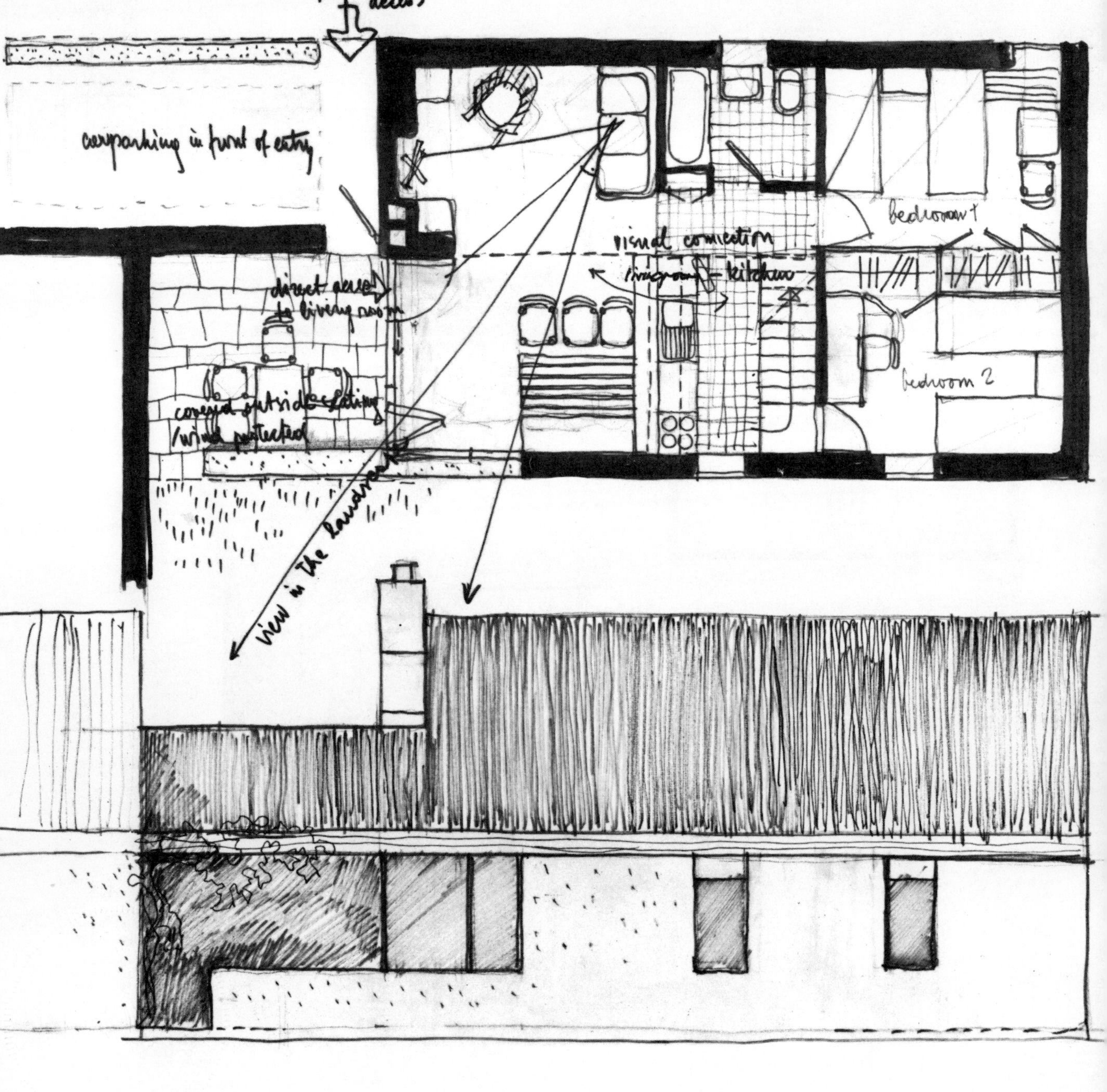

24

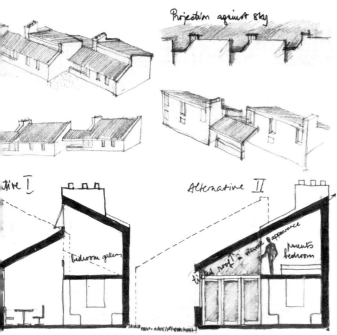

The form of the cluster of houses is such that it relates to the existing scale and method of traditional rural building without slavish copying of it.

Figure A14 shows an example. Alternative I consists of six L-shaped courtyard or patio houses fitted into the landscape at a point where a number of existing stone walls intersect. The lines of the fences are continued in the layout of the houses.

Alternative II shows a row of holiday houses with steeply sloping roofs which include an upper gallery sleeping area above ground floor living, cooking, and sleeping quarters. Four bedrooms can be provided in this way.

Houses can be joined together in a number of ways dependent on the degree to which the land slopes, the angle of summer sunlight, and

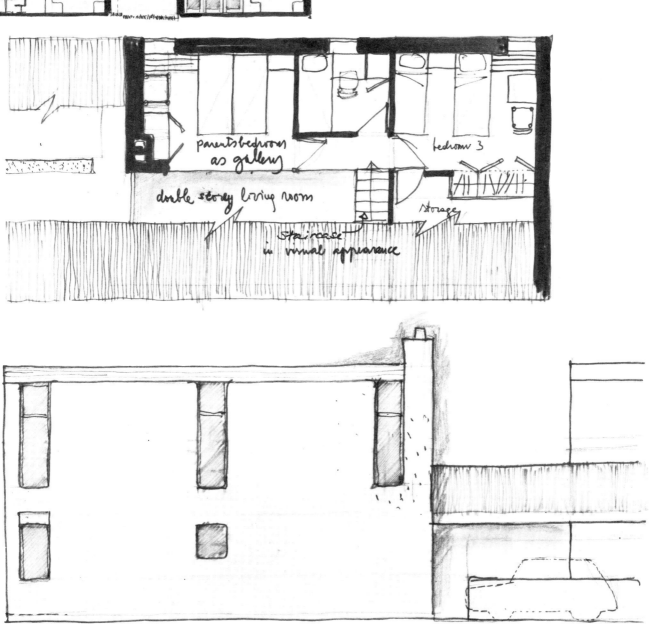

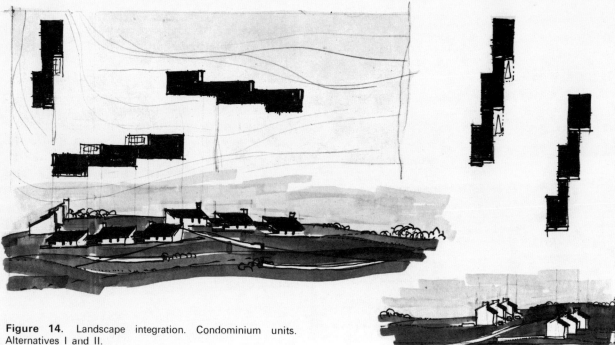

Figure 14. Landscape integration. Condominium units. Alternatives I and II.

other characteristics of the site. Alternative roof sections are shown. This design is suitable for a farm situation, provided the number of units is not great, or for building in or around an existing village.

Performance Criteria for Condominium

This checklist was developed for use by planners of condominiums. It presents the full range of criteria which must be considered and evaluated when condominiums are being developed.

Resources
1 *Financial*
Private
Loans
Shares
Regional tourism
2 *Building*
New buildings
Direct labour
Contract
3 *Operational*
Marketing
Reservations
Administration (central)
Management
Maintenance
Service and supply

Local management
Supervision
Cleaner
Back-up service
Maid
Cook
Babysitter
Maintenance
4 *Service*
Road
Water
Sewage
Waste disposal
Electricity
Telephone

Environmental
1 *Location*
Size of existing village
Siting and relationship
Appearance and character
2 *View*
Aspect
Prospect
Access
Land use
3 Cooking
Eating
Sleeping
Bathing
Recreation

Recreation and facilities
Water sports
Hunting

Shooting
Fishing
Riding
Golf
Festivals
Walking

Hotel
Retail shop
Public house and restaurant
Cinema and hall
Doctor
Church

Social

Need
    Investment in tourist
    Industry
    Prosperity
    To limit ribbon development
        at resort locations

Suitable for
    Family
    Married couples with young
        children
    Integrated into village

Accommodation
    Kitchen
    Living
    Dining
    Bedrooms 2/3
    Bathroom
    Toilets and cloakrooms
    Linen press
    Broom cupboard

Equipment
    Kitchen sink and fitting
    Cooker
    Washer (clothes)
    Refrigerator
    Iron and ironing board
    Cooking utensils
    Table ware
    Table linen

Sanitary fittings
    Shower and bath
    Wash hand-basin
    Toilets

Furniture
    Wardrobe
    Beds
    Press and shelves
    Chairs and tables

Services
    Central heating
    Hot and cold water service
    Electric fittings and lamps
    Soil and waste
    Ventilation to kitchen
    Telephone
    Car port
    Boiler installation
    Storage

COTTAGE UNITS

Rented Cottages

There is already a well-developed "rent-a-cottage" scheme in Ireland. What follows are suggestions for the design of newly built cottages and their relationship to the landscape.

Cottage Cluster

The units shown in the drawings are intended to be built in accordance with the philosophy behind the "rent-an-Irish cottage" scheme—the provision of rented holiday accommodation which will provide the maximum social and economic benefit to the inhabitants of the villages in which the cottages are sited and at the same time enable the visitor to participate in Irish rural life. It is possible to fulfil these aims without repeating directly the architecture of a bygone era.

The units are intended to be sited near the village. They are grouped closely together, so as to tie in with the existing village form and are either directly linked together or are joined by stone walls. In scale, form, and use of material, the new cottages relate to the characteristics of the existing village.

Row House and Village Extension

This type of house is intended to provide rented holiday accommodation in or adjacent to a village. It is designed to fit into the existing physical-scale of the village, and can be interlocked on plan with other houses of a similar type, so providing a variety of outline and form.

As the drawings (Figs. A15 and A16) show, the houses can be moved vertically in relation to one another in order to adjust to the contours.

This type of dwelling might also be suitable for infilling derelict sites between existing two-storey structures. In this instance single units could be used, as the design does not have any doors or windows on the gable walls.

Figure A17 shows existing buildings restored as satisfactory accommodation. Figure A18 shows linear extension element linked together and to the village.

ELEVATIONS   SECTION

ELEVATIONS

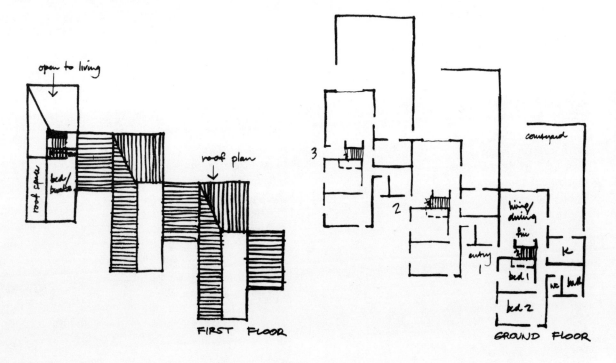

open to living

roof open

bed/bunks

roof plan

FIRST FLOOR

3

2

entry

1

courtyard

living/dining

K

bed 1

wc bath

bed 2

GROUND FLOOR

Figure A15. Village extension. Cottage scheme. Linked units.

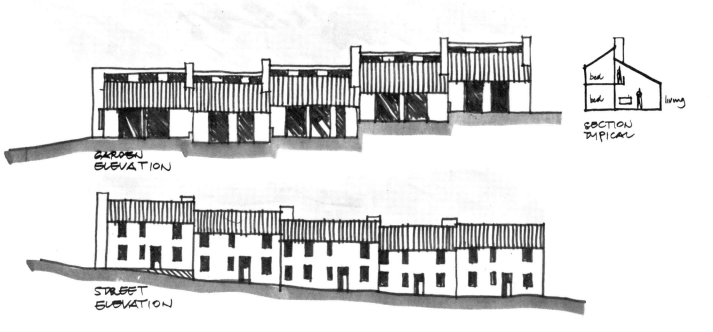

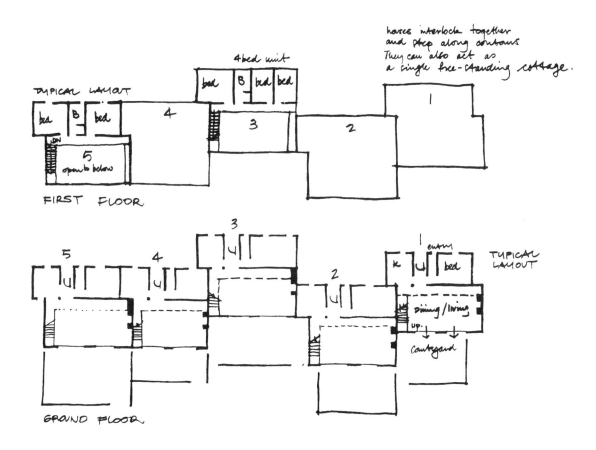

Figure A16. Village extension. Row house type 1.

Figure A17. Urban infill restoration.

Figure A18. Cottages as village extension. Linear extension elements linked together and to village.

Performance Criteria for Cottage Units

This checklist indicates all the criteria which should be taken into consideration in the development of holiday cottage units.

A, outstanding
B, good
C, acceptable

D, fair
E, unacceptable

Resources	A	B	C	D	E
1 *Financial*					
Grants					
Shares					
Loans					
Private					
Cost of development					
2 *Construction*					
Contractor					
Direct labour					
3 *Operation*					
(Central)					
Marketing					
Reservations					
Administration					
Maintenance					
Management					
Service and supply					
(Local)					
Supervision					
Cleaner					
Cooks					
Babysitters					
Maintenance					

Environmental framework	A	B	C	D	E
1 *External*					
Siting					
Appearance					
Character					
View					
Aspect					
Prospect					
Access					
2 *Internal*					
Cooking					
Eating					
Bathing					
Sleeping					
Recreation					

Recreational Relationship	A	B	C	D	E
Hunting					
Shooting					
Fishing					

	A	B	C	D	E
Coarse					
Game					
Sea					
Riding					
Instruction					
Pony trek					
Golf					
Pitch and putt					
Boating					
Festivals					
Water ski					

Social frame	A	B	C	D	E
Suited for					
Family					
Married couples					
Groups single people					
Teenagers					
Young children					
Secluded					
Integrated with village					
Accommodation					
Kitchen					
Living/dining					
Bed 1					
Bed 2					
Bed 3					
Bathroom					
Toilet					
Hot press					
Equipment					
Sink					
Cooker					
Washer					
Refrigerator					
Broom cupboard					
Ironing board					
Drawers					
Cupboards					
Pot store					
Crockery					
Shower					
Bath					
Washbasins					
Wardrobes					
Shelves					
Vanitory units					
Table					
Chairs					
Table lamps					
Heating					
Power points					

Performance Criteria for Villages with Cottage Potential Development

A, outstanding   D, fair
B, good   E, unacceptable
C, acceptable

Resources	A	B	C	D	E
1 Human					
Population structure					
Leadership potential					
Local committee					
Cultural activity					
2 Finance					
Shares					
Local authority					
Regional tourist					
Bord Failte					
Private					
3 Facilities					
Hotel					
Public House					
Restaurant					
Shops					
Village hall					
4 Services					
Water					
Electricity					
Sewerage					
Post Office and Telephone					
Refuse collection					

Environmental framework	A	B	C	D	E
1 Physical structure					
Size of village					
Density					
Degree of decay					
2 Character					
Rural					
Clean and tidy					
Irish					
3 Sites					
Location					
Relationships to:					
existing					
future					
Land use					
Price					
Availability					
Number of choices					
Planning					
Sanction					

Recreational relationship	A	B	C	D	E
Hunting					
Shooting					
Fishing					
Coarse					
Game					
Sea					
Riding					
Instruction					
Pony trek					
Golf					
Pitch and putt					
Festival					
Boating					
Water skiing					

Social framework

Need	A	B	C	D	E
Emigration rates					
Prosperity					
Existing industries					
Existing tourist					
Benefit					
Political attidue of					
Local authority					
Regional tourist					
Authority					
Bord Failte					

Group B
Transport

The work of Group B threw light on one of the major questions posed by the seminar, namely, what could be done in *design* terms to solve the special problems caused by motor traffic.

As might be expected, the group rapidly concluded that design treatment of the symptoms of the problem—the rash of badly designed or inappropriate artifacts which serve the car and which litter the countryside—is no solution, and that by attempting to deal with the causes they could make a more useful contribution.

Short of banning or restricting the use of cars and caravans they proposed a policy of dispersal in two ways, first by extending the season and reducing the seasonal peak of traffic so that congestion would be reduced, and, secondly, by encouraging deflection of tourist traffic from the fast, main traffic routes.

Other proposals were concerned with the use of natural screening and camouflage of the inevitable caravan sites, car parks, and lay-bys, and by the careful planning of these in relation to traffic routes and areas of natural beauty which should be preserved for the walker.

The Group moved on to consider the detailed design of colours and components of such things as garages, filling stations, and lay-bys.

The Group recognised that much valuable study and research had already been carried out in Ireland by people qualified to study the country's transport problems. It was felt, therefore, that the most useful plan was to try to complement this by concentrating on general principles of wide application.

The Brief

Motor-cars and caravans are inevitable concomitants to tourism yet often deface the towns and countryside being visited.

Participants were asked to study this problem and make proposals for the treatment of:

Caravan sites

Car parks

Lay-bys and picnic sites

Garages, etc.

What control should be exercised over the siting, frequency, and size of these facilities and what can be done by landscaping, component design, and colour treatment to reduce their adverse effects to a tolerable level?

It was suggested that the Group's investigation and proposals might fall into the following three parts:

1. Evaluation of, and recommendations on, the existing situation observed during field trips.

2. Design proposals for the vehicles and associated buildings and equipment encountered in the tourist area. This to include consideration of type, size, and frequency.

3. Design proposals for the siting, screening, or other treatment of vehicles and associated buildings and equipment encountered in the tourist area, including also consideration of type, size, and frequency.

The Existing Situation

At the outset the Group summarised the present position as follows:

1. In terms of travelling, Ireland is a destination not, like Germany and many other European countries, a transit country.

2. July and August are peak tourist periods in Ireland. This produces a high demand for trans-

port during the period and a contrastingly lower demand for the rest of the year. The efforts of Bord Failte (the Irish Tourist Board) to counter-act this are particularly commended.

3. The number of tourists visiting Ireland in 1971 were, in round figures:

USA	250,000
England	1,500,000
Other countries	100,000

To these figures must be added the number of Irish tourists visiting places in their own country.

4. Another factor affecting the transport system is the number of overseas tourists bringing their own cars and caravans to Ireland. In 1971, 150,000 cars entered the Republic from overseas and 70,000 came in through Northern Ireland. These are in addition to the 4000 rent-a-cars and 400 coaches permanently based in Ireland.

5. The Irish road network is planned for local business, commercial, and recreational use, but a large increase in the number of tourists over the last few years has given rise to problems of a technical, economic, aesthetic, and environ-mental nature.

Looking at the transport facilities in terms of the type of vehicle involved, the position appears to be this:

(a) Car, motor-cycle. Road network extensive, mostly in good condition and relatively under-used.

(b) Car and caravan. Small number of caravans entering the country but caravan hire facili-ties available.

(c) Dormobile. Small number entering country.

(d) Bus. (i) Good local bus service in large towns. (ii) Poor long-distance bus services.

(e) Tourist coach. Wide range of facilities avail-able.

(f) Bicycle. Hire facilities available in some areas.

(g) Train. Network leaves much of Ireland not covered. Plans exist for qualitative improve-ment but not for extension.

(h) Horse-drawn caravans. Hire facilities avail-able in certain areas.

(i) Horse. Limited pony-trekking facilities avail-able.

(j) Boat. Hire facilities available.

(k) Walking. Very few countryside paths.

Group Results

The Group saw a number of unsatisfactory aspects requiring corrective action within the existing situation.

Lack of Co-ordination at Political Level

Although there is a single authority for all major trunk roads there is no single planning authority for the overall road network. Remedial legislation is being introduced. Decisions are taken by each of the different county authorities. This can result in sudden changes of road width and surface, which can be a cause of accidents.

The lack of co-operation between the depart-ments of local councils which are in charge of car-parking facilities, on the one hand, and with the historic monuments' authority, on the other, could often result in unsympathetic juxtaposition of car park and monument.

Road Conditions

Narrow, winding roads increase the pleasure of driving so long as there is no other traffic on the road, but they are at the same time a poten-tial cause of accidents. The effect of accidents might, however, be reduced by the slower speeds which are normal on such roads.

Rest Points

Lay-bys. Much could be gained by increasing the number of lay-bys and making them more interesting. At present they consist typically of a small strip of road separated from the main highway by a narrow width of grass without screening by trees or hedges and with no change of level.

Picnic sites. Only a small number of lay-bys have been provided with seats and tables.

Car parks. Car parks which allow tourists to take advantage of scenic or historic attractions are relatively few. There seems to be little attempt to site these car parks so as not to intrude on the view.

Filling stations. Better control over the siting of filling stations and garages would seem to be necessary. They are usually to be found at the entrance and exit to most towns and villages and are often unsightly and untidy. Refreshment facilities and toilets are rare.

The existing system does not encourage the tourist to be adventurous. There is little to per-suade him to turn away for any length of time from the main roads.

Tourist Destinations

Car parks. The attention given to siting, screening, and control of car parks is insufficient and often results in a visually unsympathetic and even chaotic situation.

Caravan and camping sites. Until recently there was no control over the siting or equipment of caravan sites. A number of these haphazard and unsightly developments are still in existence. New legislation gave power to Bord Failte to refuse registration to caravan sites if they considered the siting or equipment inadequate. As yet there are few of these registered caravan sites.

Public footpaths. In recent years a number of forests have been opened to the public with a network of footpaths but these are relatively few in number. Apart from these, tourists are not made aware of the existence of public footpaths throughout the country. A system of extensive and interconnecting footpaths would encourage a greater appreciation of the countryside.

Recommendations

Signing

Signs Required

Lay-bys, intermediate stops, picnic sites. Advance signs at 1 mile, $\frac{1}{2}$ mile, $\frac{1}{4}$ mile with symbols indicating:

Parking;

View, if any;

Refreshments, if any;

Historical interest;

Scientific interest;

No heavy vehicles.

Picnic sites. Footpath signs with walking times to local destination points.

Filling stations. Advance signs required indicating services available. At the filling station—entry, exit, and thank you signs.

Destinations. Advance signs—hotel, camp, caravan, etc. Signs on site—footpath, parking, guard, open fireplace, shelter.

Lay-bys

A lay-by should not be treated merely as an emergency stop for lorry drivers or a pull-in for them. Lay-bys help to create a smooth traffic flow. They reduce the number of cars in movement on the road and give the tourist an opportunity to observe and enjoy the countryside.

Lay-bys, wherever possible, should be sited at points of interest.

In the planning of these short-term stopping places, the following points should be considered:

(a) integration of the lay-by into the surrounding landscape;

(b) separation of the lay-by from the road, possibly by a difference in levels;

(c) vehicle parking;

(d) footpaths;

(e) litter disposal;

(f) provision of information and sign-posting;

(g) picnic facilities;

(h) toilets.

Integration of the Lay-by into its Surrounding Landscape

In choosing the position for a lay-by, the planner must take into consideration the purposes for which it will be used and how well it can be made to blend into its surroundings. Large areas of hard surface are visually unsympathetic in a rural setting. These should be broken up by trees, hedges, and shrubs which are indigenous to the area. Changes of level, hedges, and walls may be used as screening.

The needs of tourists should be treated as secondary to those of residents. For this reason, items which relate to tourists should be understated, those relating to the residents emphasised.

Separation of the Lay-by from the Road

Every change in the traffic flow creates a hazardous situation and a potential accident. It is therefore necessary to design the entry and the exit to a parking place so as to reduce to a minimum the disturbance to other traffic. This can be done by providing sufficiently long connecting roads where braking and acceleration can take place.

To make it easier for the driver to stop and park his vehicle, he needs information that he is approaching a stopping place, when he can leave the road, and where he can park his car. He may also need information on how he can leave the stopping place.

Intermediate Points

An intermediate point (Fig. B1) was seen as a further development of the lay-by by providing best possibilities with additional services provided.

Vehicle Parking

It is extravagant to mark out individual parking spaces, but it may be necessary to show parking limits, and this can be done by means of embankments, planting, stone or brick walls, fences, or stones. The surface of the parking area can be of gravel, grass with stone, or concrete insets or tarmac. Usually the most practical and visually attractive solution is the use of inlaid paving blocks or stone insets, interspersed with grass.

Litter

It is necessary to provide sufficient and conveniently placed containers for litter. These should be designed for easy servicing.

Car-parking Requirements for Monuments and other Points of Special Interest

The car park may have to be a considerable distance from the place it serves if, by its sheer size, it is not to swamp what people have come to enjoy. It may even be necessary to provide frequent public transport from the car park to the site. The siting of the car park should take into account any changes of level, particularly in treeless areas.

Picnic Sites

When people want to linger, they usually choose the fringe, the line where one ecological pattern changes for another, or where bare country is interrupted by trees or rocks. They go for the hedge, the bank of a stream, the fringe line of the forest, or the woodland glade.

Considerable numbers of people want to drive their cars directly to a picnic site, and where people have come primarily to enjoy themselves, that is, to picnic rather than to enjoy fine scenery or an ancient monument. There are sites which can be planned so that people need not be separated from their cars.

Water has a very strong attraction, especially where it is possible to swim or hire a boat.

The connection between sun and slope can usefully be taken into account when shaping picnic areas.

It may be necessary to provide shade or shelter.

Figure B1. Intermediate stops.

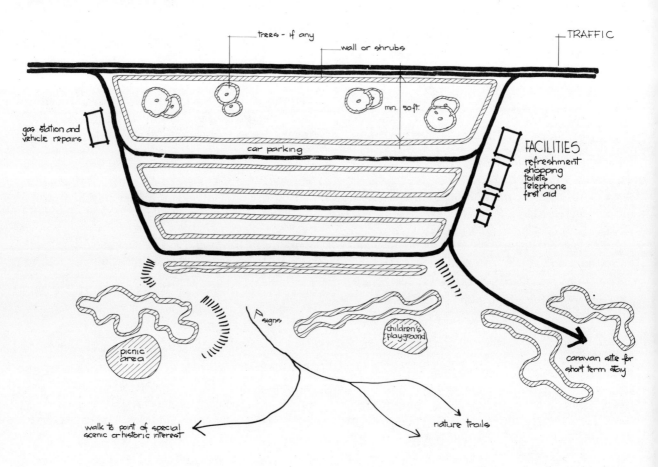

Types of Terrain

Light woodland and parkland on well-drained soil make very good picnic sites. The ease with which soil can now be shifted and semi-mature trees transplanted has changed the whole time scale of providing shelter. Small areas on the sunny fringe of a wood, taking up to half a dozen cars, could be particularly successful as picnic sites.

Forests

If forests are planned from the start for both timber production and recreation, recreation facilities may be included with little extra cost. Man's instinct to settle around the edges, together with a primitive fear of deep forest, means that as little as 5 per cent of a productive forest may be used for recreation, although the public has access to the whole forest.

Water

Pools, streams, lakes, and canals act as magnets for picknickers. Pools, in disused sand and gravel pits, can be made focal points for picnic areas.

Equipment

Benches scattered in the open with no relation to trees or planting, walls or buildings, can seem ridiculously forlorn. The space needs to be furnished in scale with itself, with benches and tables related to other parts of the design. Drinking water, fire-places, barbecues, lavatories, first-aid facilities, litter bins, and children's playgrounds should be considered.

Caravan Sites

The same criteria apply for caravan sites as for lay-bys and intermediate stops. The scale, however, is different and locations will generally be away from the main trunk routes. Figures B2 and B3 indicate the Group's thinking on the layout and land-scaping of caravan sites.

Filling Stations

In Rural Built-up Areas

The local garage on the outskirts of a rural built-up area remains from the days of the local mechanic. It has a tendency to grow and to develop distinctive characteristics. It probably contains dumps of scrap-iron and also serves as a car and tractor graveyard. It is detrimental to the image of any village since it is the first object to be noticed on entering the built-up area. Gar-

ages of this type should be discouraged, and existing ones moved to less obvious sites. They should be replaced by filling stations of a type which pays more respect to the environment.

In the Open Country

In Ireland these are rarities. Where they exist, their design is usually deplorable. They wreck the environment by their poor siting, visual disorder, their noise, and their general appearance.

In Towns and Villages

Isolated petrol pumps on the footpaths in towns and villages are a safety hazard and interrupt the traffic flow.

Figure B2. Caravan sites.

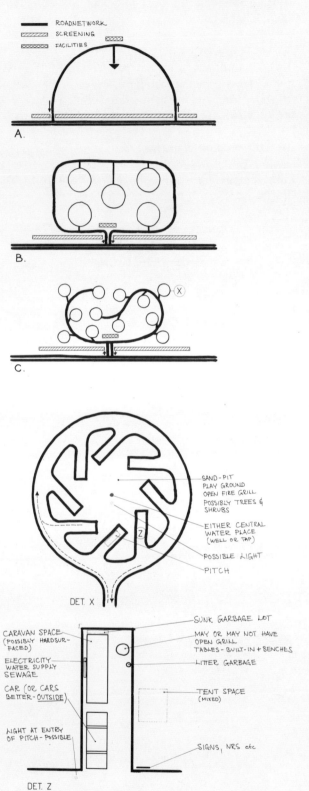

ROADNETWORK
SCREENING
FACILITIES

A.

B.

C.

SAND-PIT
PLAY GROUND
OPEN FIRE GRILL
POSSIBLY TREES &
SHRUBS

EITHER CENTRAL
WATER PLACE
(WELL OR TAP)

POSSIBLE LIGHT

PITCH

DET. X

CARAVAN SPACE
(POSSIBLY HARDSUR-
FACED)

ELECTRICITY
WATER SUPPLY
SEWAGE

CAR (OR CARS
BETTER - OUTSIDE)

LIGHT AT ENTRY
OF PITCH - POSSIBLE

DET. Z

SUNK GARBAGE LOT

MAY OR MAY NOT HAVE
OPEN GRILL
TABLES - BUILT-IN + BENCHES

LITTER GARBAGE

TENT SPACE
(MIXED)

SIGNS, NRS etc

Figure B3. Type of landscape.

TYPE OF LANDSCAPE

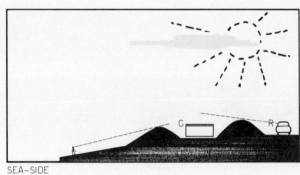

SEA-SIDE

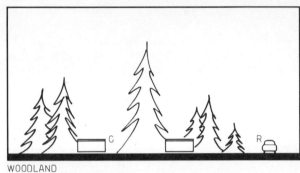

WOODLAND

C CARAVAN SITES
P CAR PARK
R ROAD
S SCREEN
B BANK

HILL-SIDE

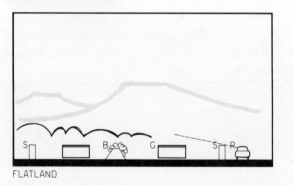

FLATLAND

Group C
General Equipment

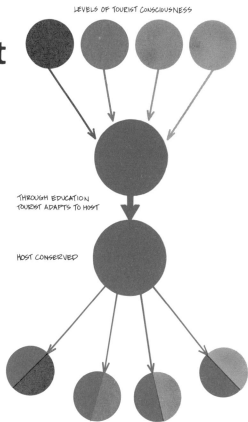

LEVELS OF TOURIST CONSCIOUSNESS

THROUGH EDUCATION
TOURIST ADAPTS TO HOST

HOST CONSERVED

NEW LEVELS OF CONSCIOUSNESS DEVELOPED

At the seaside, in the towns, and in the country-side the growth of tourism creates the need for a great deal of miscellaneous equipment such as:

Rubbish collection and disposal facilities

Lavatories

Refreshment kiosks

Information and directional signs

International signs

Seats, shelters, etc.

The Brief

Participants were asked to make a study of these items of equipment and to make proposals for them in keeping with the Irish landscape and at the same time meeting the requirements of the international tourist. Their proposals to include questions of siting, scale, colour, material, and frequency as well as such practical questions as the collection and disposal of rubbish.

The Group's investigations and proposals fall into two parts:

1. Evaluation of, and recommendations on, the existing situation as observed during field trips.

2. Specific design recommendations on items or ranges of items, together with proposals for their location and frequency.

By respecting the existing environment and improving facilities for the local residents, an atmosphere favourable to tourism is the likely result.

If the tourist is educated to a "When in Rome" attitude he is unlikely to look for special facilities, and he will tend to develop a respect and affection for his host country through this greater intimacy (Fig. C1).

Development of an educational programme was beyond the resources of the Group, but we endeavoured to indicate an attitude from which it could grow. By developing this respect and

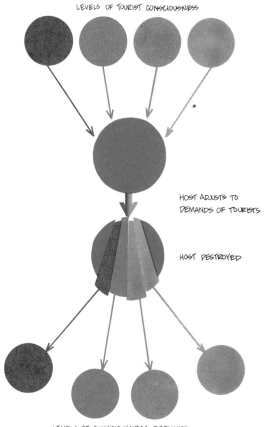

LEVELS OF TOURIST CONSCIOUSNESS

HOST ADJUSTS TO
DEMANDS OF TOURISTS

HOST DESTROYED

LEVELS OF CONSCIOUSNESS RETAINED

Figure C1.

39

affection in both resident and visitor a safeguard is built in which would help to avoid serious mistakes in judgement. To preserve the character of particular areas it is clearly desirable to avoid blanket standarisation. Wherever practicable a problem should be approached in terms of the local idiom.

Information

One of the most important facilities we can offer a tourist is information. By deciding how and when to present this information greater use can be made of existing services or those specially provided for the tourist. Many tourists choose their destination for the special and, they hope, unspoiled flavour of the host country, and want to experience its idiosyncrasies and peculiarities intact, but without discomfort. If properly prepared to meet this experience they ought to be able to join in the everyday life of the country with the minimum of disruption. Therefore, it is clearly important that adequate and accurate information be supplied, first to induce them to choose this particular holiday and then to prepare them for changed customs and situations. Once launched on their way they need a good information service, and careful attention should always be given to the siting and equipping of information bureaux. Such offices in Ireland were often difficult to find and difficult to identify. This is an instance where a strong standard identifying element would be a distinct advantage. Wherever possible, multilingual staff should be employed; the offices should reflect a regional flavour and could expand the type of information available to include contacts with local businesses and institutions and possibly include a local mini-museum. There is at present a vast quantity of repetitive and awkwardly sized printed matter offered. Streamlining and co-ordination would enable the tourist to build up a convenient reference folder.

Signposting

Many examples of misleading, difficult, and ambiguous signs were observed. Directional, informational, and utility signs could include Irish characters for the sake of atmosphere and national morale, but they should be properly designed from the point of view of legibility and recognition. For example:

Directional signs. Legible lettering, colour (blue), size (standard), shape (rectangular), arrow for direction.

Informational. Park signs, view point, etc.— same as directional but different colour (green).

Utility signs. Toilets, telephone, post-box— smaller, symbolic, different colour.

The placing, frequency, and arrangement of signs must be carefully considered. Where possible they should be placed well in advance of the point where any action is required. Many studies have been carried out and published in this area, including the International Agreement on Road Signs, Warboy's Report in England, Henry Dreyfus' *Symbols,* Heller's *Strassen, Zeichen and Symbolen,* and Richardson Hobbs' *Traffic Engineering.*

General Equipment

Rather than engage in actual product design the team felt it would be more useful to suggest general principles to be followed. Some references to particular examples are, however, necessary.

A Graph (Fig. C2) was devised which showed a method by which new design performance criteria could be established for equipment. It describes the interrelationship of permanent, mobile, and non-use elements with their environment:

1. Permanent equipment means that which is fixed or stationary, functional, and intrinsic to its surroundings.

2. By mobile is meant those units or elements which are stored, maintained, and used by local or regional authorities. They are used at occasional, seasonal, and specific times. As often as not, equipment for temporary use is permanently affixed (without discretion or plan) to the landscape, causing unnecessary economic waste and visual pollution.

3. By "not needed" or non-use is meant that the equipment is not necessary to the function of the environment.

Our basic overall policy of implementation suggested *no* manmade intrusions in the environ-

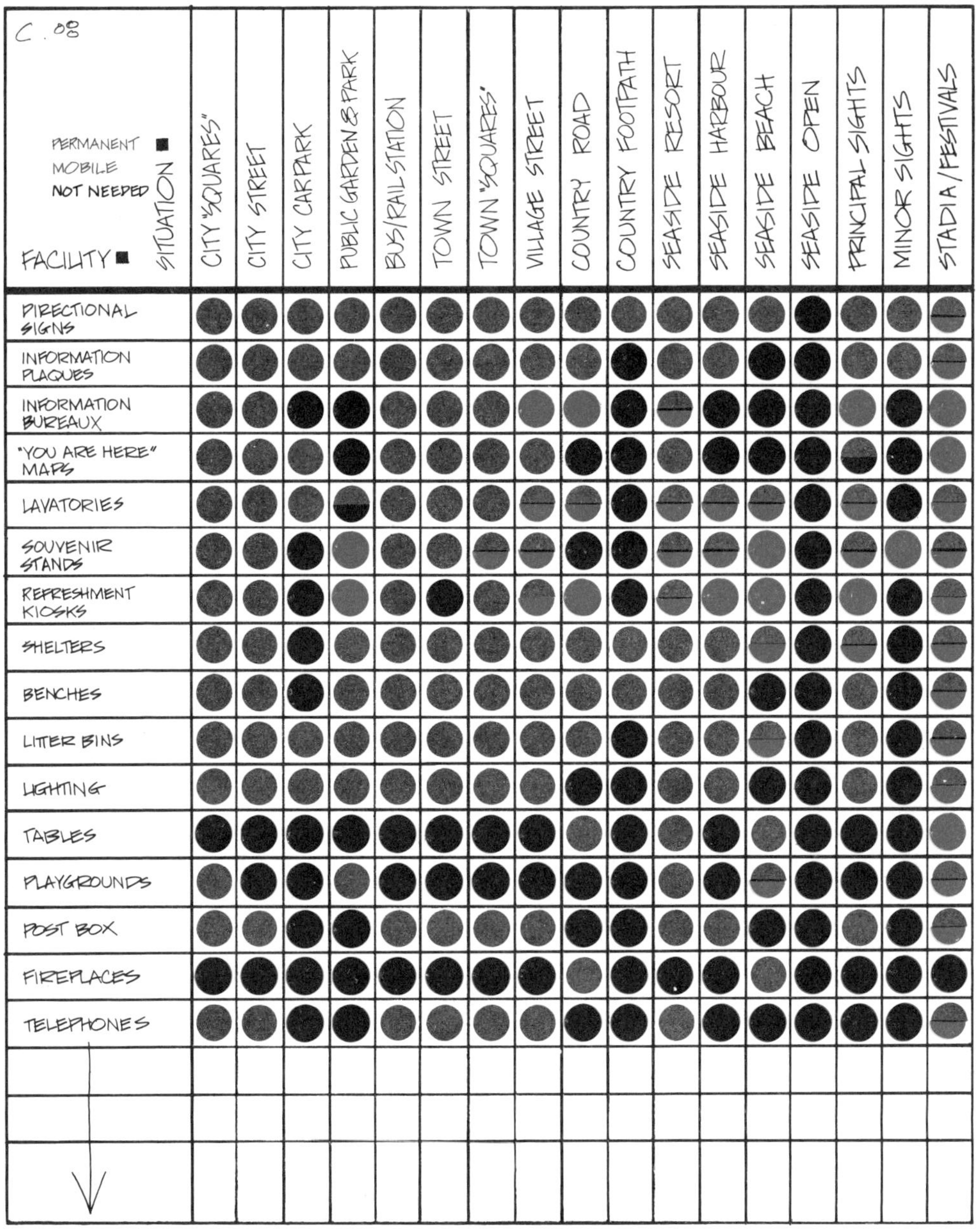

C.08

PERMANENT ■
MOBILE ●
NOT NEEDED

FACILITY ■ SITUATION

Column headers (situations): CITY "SQUARES" · CITY STREET · CITY CARPARK · PUBLIC GARDEN & PARK · BUS/RAIL STATION · TOWN STREET · TOWN "SQUARES" · VILLAGE STREET · COUNTRY ROAD · COUNTRY FOOTPATH · SEASIDE RESORT · SEASIDE HARBOUR · SEASIDE BEACH · SEASIDE OPEN · PRINCIPAL SIGHTS · MINOR SIGHTS · STADIA/FESTIVALS

Row labels (facilities): DIRECTIONAL SIGNS · INFORMATION PLAQUES · INFORMATION BUREAUX · "YOU ARE HERE" MAPS · LAVATORIES · SOUVENIR STANDS · REFRESHMENT KIOSKS · SHELTERS · BENCHES · LITTER BINS · LIGHTING · TABLES · PLAYGROUNDS · POST BOX · FIREPLACES · TELEPHONES

Figure C2.

ment except where absolutely appropriate and necessary.

Items such as refuse baskets, post-boxes, lighting, seating, and playgrounds, need closer attention. The variation in style and colour, and the placing of refuse baskets is so great that they are often hard to find and to recognise. Post-boxes, because of their colour (green), type (free-standing or mounted on walls), and placing (behind corners, in between doorways, in flat walls, along alleys, and roads), are particularly hard to find and may be confused with water hydrants or refuse containers. A change of colour to yellow or orange would greatly help, and so would signs showing where they may be found. The labelling on post-boxes showing times of collections should be larger and clearer. A complete solution can only be achieved through a total redesign of the system.

Street lighting is arranged with little consideration of the traffic requirements or of the character of the area. We observed that in some areas two different types of lamp were mounted together, apparently to increase the intensity of the lighting. This increased the jumble of wires, posts, and signs. On small streets where subdued lighting would be desirable, white lamps have been installed, causing over-illumination. If in any particular area there were no more than four types of lamp, the improvement would be great. The lighting of signs and the use of flood lighting of historic buildings should be encouraged.

ENNIS PILOT STUDY

The Group chose the town of Ennis for a pilot study to explain by way of illustration many of its recommendations.

Our object was to explore the town with a view to developing the character already there rather than to suggest sweeping and expensive changes. Emphasis is placed on small-scale projects which one could expect local communities to organise and that demonstrate how such schemes enhance the town itself.

Ennis is the county town of Clare—a principal market centre and a logical centre for touring the main attractions of the county. It is a pleasant town to explore (Fig. C3)—a maze of lanes and narrow streets full of interesting commercial congestion lead into market places, small public spaces, the Abbey ruins, and, inevitably, to the river which runs through the centre of the town.

The main emphasis is centred on the River Fergus. In common with many Irish towns and villages, Ennis is built with its back turned on the river, and so a principal attraction is ignored and wasted. The town is fortunate in that a great length of the riverbank has been opened up through demolition, but only to provide car-parking space instead of emphasising the river itself.

We propose that the two existing car parks

Figure C3. Street plan of Ennis.

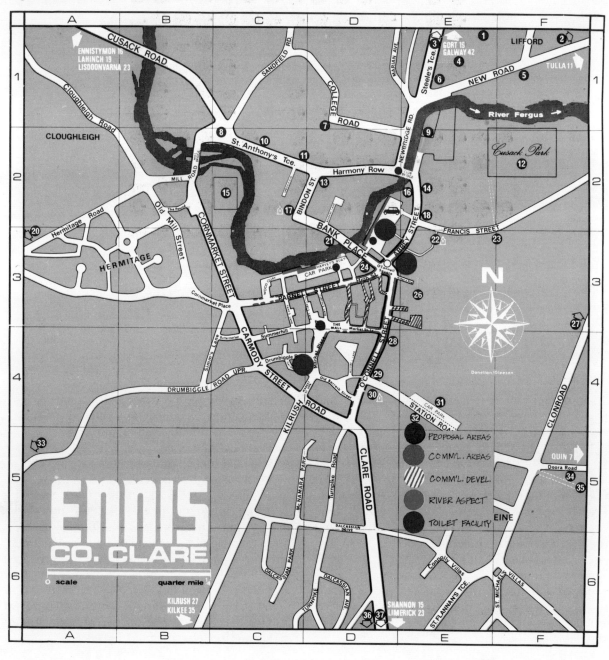

42

be adapted, with little sacrifice of capacity, to include a continuous promenade—taking advantage of the riverside aspect—a strip of about 8–10 feet wide, repaved, planted with large trees, and supplied with benches and bins (Fig. C4). The down-river end to be expanded into a small park area which would include the near-derelict buildings as a playground and child-minding centre and a possible petrol-service station. The strip would ideally extend even *through* existing buildings as far up the river as Mill Road.

We also propose that Club Bridge be developed along existing lines with the platforms simplified and extended with benches set into the river wall to encourage greater use (Fig. C5). The Memorial would thus be given greater importance in its new space with the elimination of fussy shapes and structures. This would have obvious benefits for the local population. If the derelict mills near the tennis club were converted

Figure C5.

Ennis: 1916 Memorial, Club Bridge

Ennis: Market Place and The Mall

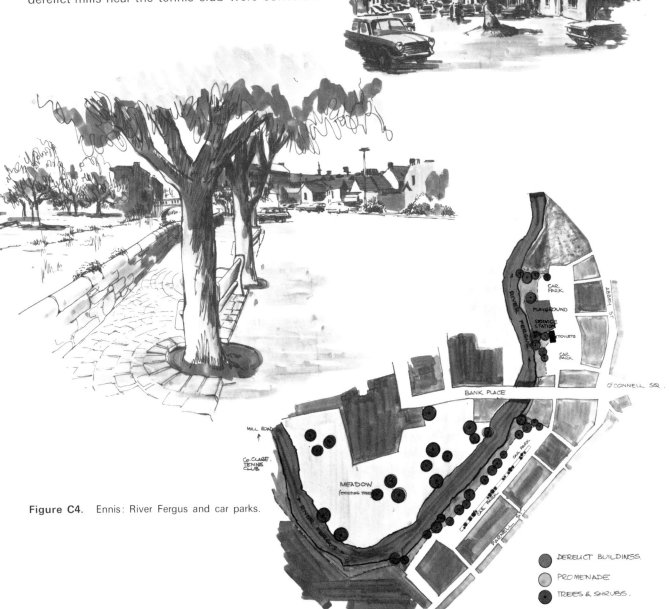

Figure C4.   Ennis: River Fergus and car parks.

43

into hotel accommodation, a pleasant pedestrian access to the town centre would be provided for tourists.

We suggested the tidying up of the Market Place and The Mall (Fig. C5). By (a) setting back and minimising the intrusive toilet block to reveal an attractive row of cottages, and (b) removing or reducing the roundabout. This suggestion would create a focal point serving the same spatial function of the old market crosses.

It was also proposed to re-establish O'Connell Square and the Monument as the principle activity area of the town after noticing that the towns-people gathered there throughout the day

Figure C6.   Ennis: O'Connell Square.

(Fig. C6). The proposals were to re-site the Information Office plus a "you are here" map on the Abbey Street corner with a new toilet block below. The eastern side could be exploited as a seating area taking into consideration the local custom of sitting on the Monument base. A telephone and post-box should be added. Flat cupped trees at the top end of the blank eastern wall, dressed with a vine, would utilise the seasonal colour changes. The surrounding buildings would incorporate restaurants and cafes to maintain activity beyond normal business hours. With the addition of some landscaping, an attractive oasis could be formed, again to the great benefit of the local people and the visitor.

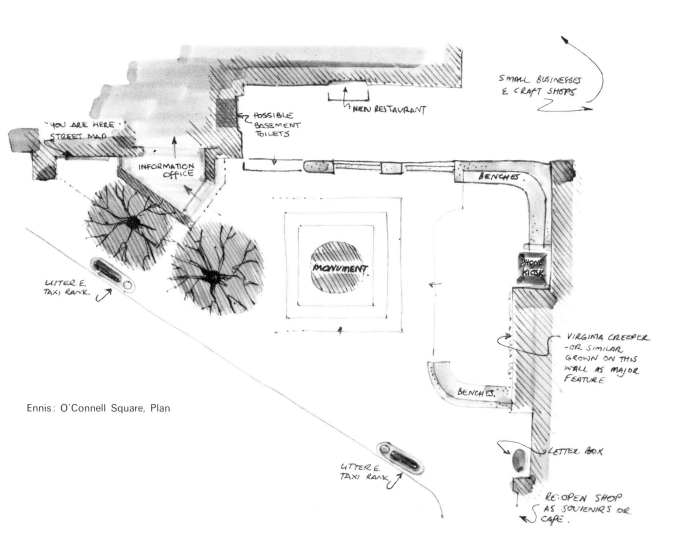

Ennis: O'Connell Square, Plan

Group D
Colour and Materials

The brief required an examination of the more intangible qualities of the Irish landscape and the presentation of these in a form which could guide designers working in Ireland. Design briefs were mainly composed of instructions concerning the quantifiable aspects of a project. The problem of specifying qualitative values is a real one which has rarely been solved.

The team carried out a detailed survey of the nature of the landscape and translated this material into a series of diagrammatic drawings which tried to convey the essence of the landscape in graphic terms. The text which accompanies these drawings identifies certain general principles which go to determine the whole visual quality of the landscape yet whose influence is not always recognised or appreciated. These principles lie at the root of the work of designers and architects.

Children and Landscape

Children are the tourists of the future. They deserve consideration now. They should be made aware of their environment, for it is through the education of the young that the tourist of the future is formed.

A series of folded paper games was designed to encourage children in observation and enjoyment of the countryside. This idea has potentialities in many countries of the world, being inexpensive to implement and being of enormous value in educating children in the appreciation and conservation of the countryside.

The Brief

The particular characteristics of a region are partly atmospheric and climatic but are also composed of the colours, materials and forms of the natural landscape and indigenous structures. A study was suggested of these characteristics in relation to the landscape of Ireland so that general proposals could be formulated for ranges of colour and materials which should be used in new buildings or structures which were to be erected in the region.

Participants were asked to carry out such a study and to prepare general recommendations on the use of colour and materials.

Analysis of the Brief

The Group felt that it should be concerned not only with the appearance of the natural landscape but more with the fact that the country is a living organism that must be considered as a whole.

Industrial development and modern travel disturb the balance by introducing elements that are out of scale. Tourism and temporary residents who have no vital attachment to the region also disturb this balance.

Industry and tourism usually involve large-scale financial investment. Such investments are not easily regulated. On the other hand, damage to the natural balance can go beyond the point of no return.

If new manmade elements which modify the landscape are to be introduced, these elements should proceed from the organic whole, by being born from it, and so fit into the life of the region.

The Group re-defined the project in more precise terms as follows:

1. To make information available to local inhabitants, national and foreign tourists, that would make them aware and respectful of the country

by showing how the beauty of the landscape is the result of all ecological interactions into a unique, well-balanced organism.

2. To create a tool that will help local authorities, designers, architects, and persons responsible for local equipment, conservation, and information, to be conscious of the country as an organic whole, so that the result of their work should be born from an understanding of this total organism.

Analysis of the General Landscape

Attention was paid principally to the constant features of each distinctive region, noting the characteristic elements.

Travel was perceived as a continuous experience of landscape and surroundings in contrast with place to place movement (tourism).

Landscape was perceived related to movement in space (wind, clouds, waves) and in time (light, hours, seasons).

The Group attempted to understand the interactions and relations of the observable elements as an organic living whole.

Attention was given to the fact that the distinctive aesthetic quality of a region or landscape was due to the constants and not to the exceptional elements, to the life as a whole, to changes of light and atmosphere.

These constants were grouped and distinguished as follows:

Atmosphere. Prevailing wind; Light; Weather

Geology. Kind of rock; Slant of rock layers; Colour, quality or soil; General line of hills; Rivers; Beaches

Botany. Plant life at different levels—wild and planted

Human elements. Roads—paths; Gates, stiles, bridges; Canals, harbours, fords

Farming. Crops—sizes, types, and situation of fields; Animals; Hedges and fences; Carts, tools, haystacks, manure heaps

Architecture. Walls; Cottages; Farms and barns; Colour on buildings; Materials

Sports and leisure.

Examples of external, intrusive, non-constant elements. Industrial buildings; Signs; Rubbish, litter; Electric poles; Mining; Hotels

Assumption

That tourism is about Ireland's own people. Ireland should aim at attracting the type of tourist which will appreciate, respect, and have sympathy for the people and the country.

Behind the Landscape

To be able to appreciate a country you need to understand why it is as it is.

Usually only the most *un*usual things are pointed out to tourists—castles, monuments, and specially shaped or picturesque rocks or mountains.

Attention should rather be given to characteristic features which may not necessarily be seen as interesting by local people. These closely interlinked characteristics should be regarded as a whole:

Climate	Sites of villages
Geology	Plant and animal life
Crops and cattle	Industry
Architecture	Roads

In other words we should begin by observing the constants of the landscape in an area. We should try to understand the internal mechanics of these constants or understand how they are linked together to form a whole. We should try to explain how future developments and equipment can fit into that whole by internal logic.

Analysis of Landscape: Constants

The following analysis can be used by the responsible authorities, designers, and architects as a checklist when introducing new equipment in a given environment.

This list is not meant to be complete but to help in an analysis of the environment by pointing out some typical Irish elements and by demonstrating their aesthetic and ecological value.

47

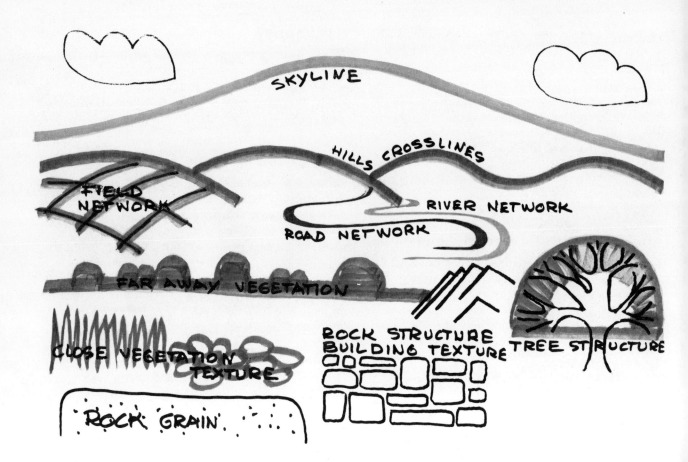

Figure D1. Structural Lines of Landscape

The observer distinguishes different structures at different distances.

The skyline is usually a continuous soft line with no indentation after it has been softened by atmosphere, rain, and mist.

The profile of the hills will give a crossing pattern of broken colours.

The forestry and field structure will be rectangular or curved following the size and the tilt of the hills.

The network of paths and roads.

Far-away vegetation. The profile of the hedges. Isolated trees. The different colours of trees in woods. The profile pattern of trees in woods.

The rock pattern. The tilt and fragmentation of a rock pattern.

The inner field pattern. Furrows. Crop-rows.

Trees. Their inner pattern of trunk and branches. Ivy on trees and walls.

The building pattern of roofs and walls.

The close vegetation pattern of leaves.

Stonework and brickwork.

The grain of stone.

Rivers, streams, highways, and electric wires can be considered as links between the other features of the landscape.

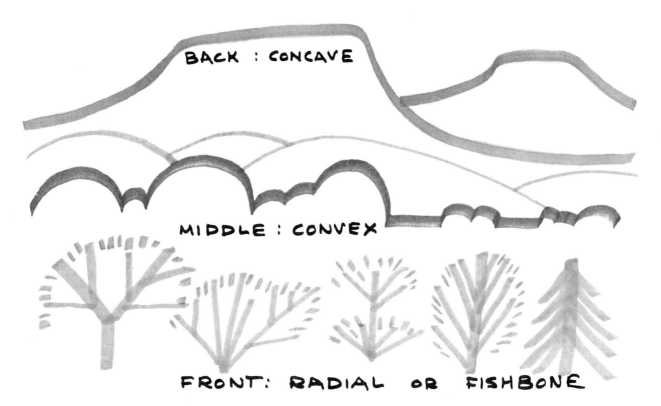

BACK : CONCAVE

MIDDLE : CONVEX

FRONT: RADIAL OR FISHBONE

Figure D2. Constants in Structural Lines

Mountains on the skyline usually have concave lines.

Smaller hills, wood, and tree profiles are usually convex, with the dominant shapes of oak, beech, and willow. Spruce will give jagged vertical, and pine jagged horizontal, lines.

The inner tree structure will be more apparent in the foreground as a fishbone or radial structure.

Buildings.

Figure D3. Broken Lines

The structural and geological lines of land are usually softened by vegetation, by the profile of irregular hedgerows, and of wood with mixed kinds of trees. Manmade elements will blend in the same way if their profile is made to avoid long, straight lines.

We notice the broken line of roofs, chimneys, the jagged topping of walls, vegetation growing on walls, creepers on walls, and angles.

Figure D4. Constant Colour

The use of a constant material or colour or module will help to integrate different sizes and forms of buildings into a coherent landscape.

50

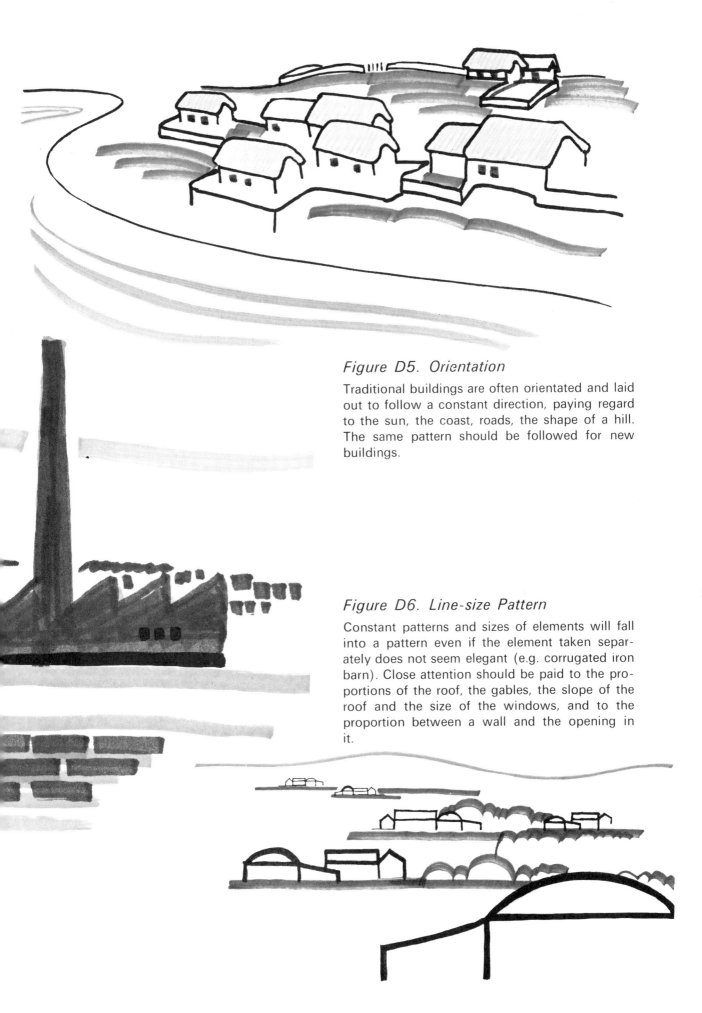

Figure D5. Orientation

Traditional buildings are often orientated and laid out to follow a constant direction, paying regard to the sun, the coast, roads, the shape of a hill. The same pattern should be followed for new buildings.

Figure D6. Line-size Pattern

Constant patterns and sizes of elements will fall into a pattern even if the element taken separately does not seem elegant (e.g. corrugated iron barn). Close attention should be paid to the proportions of the roof, the gables, the slope of the roof and the size of the windows, and to the proportion between a wall and the opening in it.

51

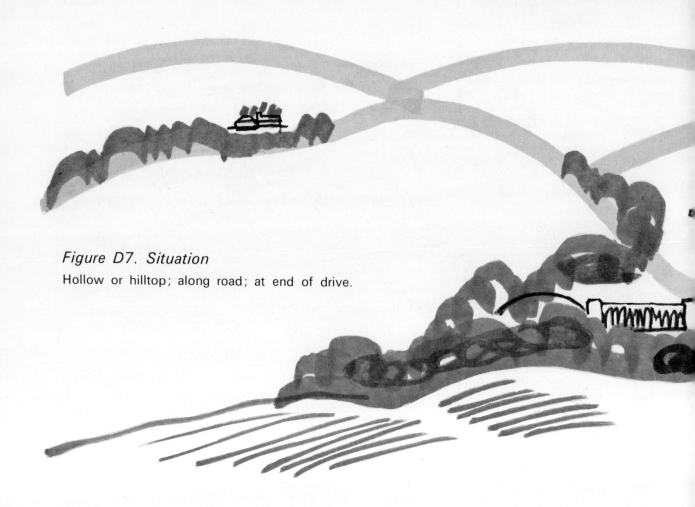

Figure D7. Situation

Hollow or hilltop; along road; at end of drive.

Figure D8. Proportion of Bright Colour

The proportion of bright colour in a landscape should be kept at the usual low level according to the:

Size of object

Intensity of colour

Contrast on background

Distance it will be seen from, and permanence

For example, a brightly coloured circus will be accepted (as non-permanent) but, in the same place a smaller bright, permanent advertisement would be unacceptable.

An isolated brightly painted building will be good in a large open landscape and bad in a restricted area.

52

Figure D9. Proportions of Buildings

The proportions of traditional buildings in a landscape are usually constant. To keep new buildings in accordance with this constant the following guidelines are helpful:

1. If a higher building has to be created, the height and width and general proportion of visible walls should be kept within approximately the same value.

2. If a longer proportion is chosen it could be fragmented into smaller sections joined together. Roofs being less conspicuous could be flat or low for such large buildings as hotels and factories.

Figure D10. Buildings on Skyline

Traditional buildings usually do not stand out against the skyline. If they do, they are surrounded by trees or high hedges that break the short lines of walls and roofs.

Figure 11. Wind Influence: A Constant

The dominant wind influences vegetation by bending trees in one direction, lengthening the profile, breaking the symmetry of the tree structure, and making tree trunks wavy instead of straight. Small woods and thickets appear much more like single masses, with a more continuous outline always slanting on the same side, and, after slanting up from the ground, affording continuity with the ground skyline.

Buildings are usually situated in the lea of the wind—kept close to the ground—and protected by low walls. New buildings should conform to these standards.

Building Materials: A Constant

Stone. Old buildings set in the landscape were built of stone or other local materials and blend with the landscape, especially where the local rock is apparent. The older the building the better the stones are chosen and joined. Hewn-stone building is more of an art than cut stone, and cut-stone building has at all times been considered as specially skilled labour. *An architect has never built a wall*. The visual effect of pattern created by good masonry is more important than the stone itself as a material. Stone should only be used in new buildings if a very skilled workman is available. If not, it should only be used as pavement or large-scale cladding. One should not try to mimic masonry by sticking sliced stone on cement.

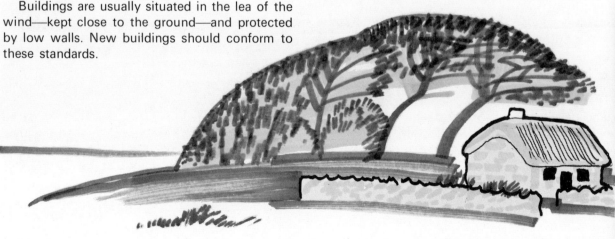

In a rock or mountain environment, stones used for building non-constant equipment should follow as much as possible the natural pattern and strata of the local rock.

Boundary walls should be built without too much mortar to allow fern masses and plants to colonise it. Stone will help lichen growth.

Limestone, sandstone, and granite will change the value of colour contrast against vegetation. The constant should be observed.

Wood. Wood is not prominent in Irish building except in details such as fences, benches, posts, and electric poles. It could be used for public equipment (benches, shelters, etc.) and would weather faster than other materials and blend into the landscape by turning grey. Wood could be used for building as a new constant in wooded country and in secluded areas.

Asbestos. Asbestos should be preferred to corrugated iron for roofing as it will allow the growth of lichens.

Corrugated iron. Corrugated iron for barns has become such a constant in the Irish landscape that it has acquired citizenship.

The red protective paint makes a pleasant contrast with the green background but it does not blend as do slate roofs.

If metallic protection is used on corrugated iron, preference should be given to the matt kind that gives a softer pattern. If it is too glossy it will give unpleasant reflections in certain kinds of light.

Thatch. Thatch is a fairly common feature in the Irish landscape. It provides very soft outlines, and the silvery colour will fit very well into the natural pattern. If this is used for new buildings it should be kept for those not larger than the average farm or cottage.

Concrete Blocks. Concrete block walls will, with time, gather moss and lichens. The colour will be rather similar to limestone, but the regular pattern of joints should not be emphasised by too much or too clear mortar. Its graining will give good light effect with whitewash.

For walls, blocks left without topping will gather soil in their hollows—plants will be able to grow in them and soften the sharp and straight outline against the background.

Cast concrete. In using cast concrete one should avoid over-large flat surfaces. Surfaces can be grained by sandblasting or hammering. Structural beams and columns should express their function by leaving the marks of the shuttering boards visible.

Macadam. This should be avoided on drives, lay-bys, and parking spaces as its dark colour does not fit well into the natural environment. It also absorbs and radiates too much heat in summer. Surfacing and pavement in areas where traffic is not intense should allow some growth of short vegetation.

Figure D12. Isolated Trees: A Constant

Isolated trees are a very striking constant feature for the continental visitor. More tree planting should be done in Ireland, especially in developing areas. Tree stumps are usually left in place and after a while make very good natural features.

Figure D14. Mixed Kinds of Trees: A Constant

In woods and hedges many different kinds of trees mingle to give different values of green and different qualities of transparency. Commercial forestry tends to change this by monoculture of resinous trees, usually spruce or pine, which affect the landscape by giving it sharper and more geometric outlines and patterns. This could sometimes be corrected by planting lower-growing trees and shrubs on the edges of the woodland. Trees can provide a transition line to open country and useful protection from strong winds. This monoculture, especially of spruce, may affect plant and animal life in these areas very strongly. Close-planted spruce will eliminate all other plant life and, if planted too close to a stream, spruce will absorb too much water and eliminate trout and other fish because of the deep shadow which the trees cast.

Figure D15. Drives, Gates, Stiles: A Constant

Drives leading to mansions or large farmhouses are usually bare, not planted with trees, and curved to follow the natural curves of the grounds.

Gates with low, massive, stone gateposts are usually made of iron, of a simple local pattern, and painted with red protective paint. Over-designing should be avoided here. Wood could be used more often, but processed—not painted.

Figure D16. Sanctuaries

Mountain tops
Historical sites
Bird and plant sanctuaries

Outstanding places in the landscape and environmental should be kept absolutely intact. In bird and plant sanctuaries, where human intervention would disturb the natural balance, access should be forbidden. Roads should not give cars or coaches access to mountain tops or go too close to viewpoints or historic sites. Large macadam or concrete parking spaces should be especially avoided These sites should be reached by walking at least the last stage, as in a pilgrimage. A careful choice of parking space, or vegetative screening, should keep these amenities out of the picture altogether.

The surrounding areas should be clearly outlined to prevent any unsightly building or change in the environment. All commercial activity should be forbidden in these areas.

Roads made only for the purpose of tourism

are usually very harmful to the natural environment.

Drives or parking spaces could be made of pierced concrete slabs, allowing the growth of mosses and grass, or pebbles can be set on end on a concrete base, allowing soil and vegetation to collect in the spaces in between. The spaces can be paved with stones with large gaps left between them.

Water-towers, when needed, should be of simple form or massive outline, not on stilts, and be everywhere of a type, size, and colour to fit into the environment. Dark or light-grained concrete should be used to blend in with either local stone or whitewash. When repeated, this form will become part of the constant human context of landscape, like church spires and corrugated iron barns.

New Building: Non-Constant

To be considered when planting the area surrounding a hotel:

Site—hilltop, valley, lowland, mountain slope, sea front

General lines of landscape

Constant lines of area landscape

Dominant wind

Force of wind

Quality and depth of soil

Kind or rocks

Drainage of soil

Screening from nearby roads and houses

Need for shelter from wind, sun, noise, rain, in different areas and directions around buildings

Rest areas

Parking spaces

Drive

Integration with Natural Features

Materials and processes, building techniques, and time planning should be studied to allow a biological integration of manmade elements in the natural picture by lichens and mosses, ferns, wall and rock plants, creepers and vines, shrubs and trees.

Shrubs and trees have to be planted, but others will grow by themselves if allowance is made during the building for their natural needs. This involves paying attention to: cracks in wall, rough surfacing, wall topping with hollows for soil, use of suitable mortar, avoiding metal, bird nesting.

Natural Camouflaging: Screening

Trees and shrubs will afford good screening for unsightly elements of landscape. Trees and shrubs provide protection against:

Sight

Noise

Sun

Wind

Rain

Air pollution

Smell

Castles and Mansions

These are usually surrounded by high trees of varying size, shape, and colour. They are often situated in a prominent position—a hilltop, an estuary, a valley threshold. Judicious placing of trees will fuse the profile of the building into the skyline. This policy should be followed for hotels when situated in prominent places. The planting of trees, hedges, and shrubs should be the first thing to be done when the site has been decided upon.

Architectural Heritage

One should aim at the conservation of the character of certain selected areas where a large proportion of the buildings were constructed during a significant architectural period or have a special association with the history of the community, state, or nation. These would normally occur in urban areas, but special groupings or isolated buildings in rural areas should also be included. This form of conservation is recognised in many countries, and the Council of Europe has recommended the preservation and development of ancient buildings and historic or artistic sites.

Such areas require very careful study and selection to permit normal urban growth and development. The importance of each building or group must be decided on in accordance with such recommendations as those set out in the Protection of the National Heritage by An Foras Forbartha (1969).

Mining in the Landscape

With the current development of mining in Ireland, one of the problems which faces the companies concerned is that of leaving the countryside as useful and pleasant-looking after the minerals have been extracted as it was before. In some cases it may even be possible to improve the appearance of the landscape.

The fact that most of the present mining proposals in Ireland are on tourist routes makes their ultimate appearance a major consideration.

The fact that in some cases a lake will be formed as a result of mining activity would suggest that some special fishing use could be made of the resulting stretch of water. The surrounding area, if planted, could possibly become a game or bird sanctuary. The future amenity value of such an area need not be compromised.

Litter in Fields

Particular attention should be given to the disposal of plastic bags used in larger and larger quantities for fertilizer and cattle feed. These are often kept in the field. If piled up, they kill all plant life under them. They are sometimes used to cover manure heaps and silos. They are blown away by the wind and consequently deface hedges and fences, fall in rivers and lakes, and can be dangerous on roads.

Some way of avoiding this could be found, for example, a discount by the factory for returning empty bags. Instructions for collecting or to destroy the bags should be printed on them.

Tourist Children and Environmental Education

The emphasis with children should be on discovery: many tourist children will see things abroad that they cannot see in their own country; perhaps things that have disappeared from there. They should be made aware that this is so.

Children should be shown at school the things they have in their own street, town, and countryside, and be taught to appreciate them.

Educational Aids for Tourist Children: Some Suggestions

1. During the journey by air: a book to read about the country, where it is in the world, etc.; a colouring book. These could be sponsored by the airline.

2. On the train and boat: information posters, e.g. "Look for these things in Ireland"—not just travelogue photographs and advertisements for hotels, etc.; books and maps to draw on.

3. (a) Tourist children's books using constants, e.g. roads, rivers, shore, in a fold-out series in order to point out the general aspects of the countryside and the build-up of the landscape, for example:
Follow the road
Follow the river
Follow the railway
Follow the postman (townscape)
Follow the shore

(b) Another series of leaflets or books on the "I spy" system, e.g. Have you seen a . . . ? This could take the form of a checklist, or spaces to write in what has been seen. The items could include: birds, flowers, insects, bridges, roads, houses, streams, rivers, lakes, sea, dunes, rocks, shore, sea.

(c) Discover cards. These cards have a built-in surprise for young children. They each have a secret and are designed to encourage children to inquire into things, e.g. to lift up stones, turn over leaves and look into trees, and to discover new things.

(d) Pop-ups and fold-ups. These are for very young children. A series of these could be developed opening apples, flowers, beehives, clouds, once again with surprise element. These could be supplied at such places as petrol stations, ferry points.

(e) Route map from point to point or city to city, showing general landscape in simple pictorial form. This must not be too complex, as car travel and book reading do not mix.

(f) Panoramic map: the general landscape of particular section of Ireland, e.g. south-east, showing physical features, vegetation, flowers, main places of interest, e.g. harbours, which open out into a full panorama.

Hotel Facilities for Children

Facilities for children to play in hotels are almost non-existent. When children do appear to have been considered, the solutions are very stereotyped and hotels often rely on entertainments provided elsewhere, e.g. seaside resorts, pin tables, fair grounds, which do not allow for creative play. It should not be assumed that when a child is on holiday he stops playing. In fact at this time a child is totally free to explore and experience new things. Neither should it be assumed that because a child is on holiday he cannot learn.

For example, a typical play area at one of the hotels visited was a sterile collection of plastic and metal, as much an eyesore as the building it was attached to. The materials used bore no relationship to the countryside around and no attempt was made to introduce children to their immediate surroundings. It was an adult's answer to how he thought a child should play. Natural materials, e.g. wood, stone, pebbles, and water, would make the play area an adventure rather than just an assembly of the same things as they would find in the park at home. A pictorial map of the immediate area would encourage children to explore the grounds; it would be rather like a treasure map. Emphasis should be on exploring and discovering.

Inside the hotel there should be one room set aside for children on rainy days. One wall could be a blackboard and there should be paints, construction toys, and pictures and charts of flowers and birds of Ireland. This might be a satisfactory alternative to the usual practice of running around the hotel.

Airport Facilities

There should be an area set aside in the terminal where children can amuse themselves in full view of parents. It could contain, for example, blackboard walls, climbing constructions, pictures, bricks, etc. During delays and while waiting for departure, there is usually nothing for the children to do, nowhere for them to go. They become disinterested in the airport soon after arrival and then rush round in all directions.

Consideration for Parents with Young Children

Hotels might consider hiring out pushchairs to guests with small children. There is seldom room in a car full of luggage for a pushchair. They might also consider keeping bicycles for the use of their guests, both adults and children. This would apply particularly to rural and seaside hotels. Information should be available about short walks and rides.

The attitude towards travel with very young or infant children is changing drastically. Once, if a child was young the parents did not travel very far. Nowadays families with very small children do travel long distances, and while hotels do make provision for this in catering, etc., there are very few other facilities available to the mother travelling with a young baby. Hotels should include changing facilities with a table, tissues, etc.

INVOLVEMENT OF CHILDREN IN THEIR OWN COUNTRY

School Projects

They should be made aware of the history of their own street, village, town, county, and country. Detailed information could be given to the older children about the areas of local historical interest so that they can act as guides during the summer holidays. They could even take responsibility for certain aspects of tourist information. In this way, by seeing that others are interested in their town they are encouraged to widen their knowledge and develop a sense of pride in what is theirs.

Further activities to which children can contribute to the benefit of residents and tourists include the following:

(a) have litter campaigns and clean-up operations;

(b) tree-planting and flower-growing competitions;

(c) competitions to identify trees, birds, insects, and flowers.

Children should be discouraged from taking birds' eggs and destroying plant life.

This can only be done by showing them what happens, giving reasons. It is not good enough just to tell them not to do this kind of action; destructive qualities come quite naturally. They should be encouraged to watch birds and to identify flowers and trees, but to leave them where they are.

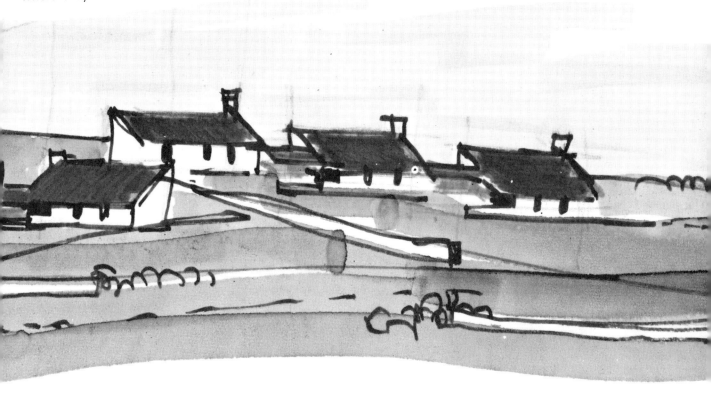

List of Participants

Australia:

DARYL JACKSON:
Partner in Melbourne firm of architect-planners, employing 20 architects. Has worked in Britain and United States. Mainly concerned with planning educational and recreational facilities in Australia and Fiji.

Austria:

DOMINIC HABSBURG LOTHRINGEN:
Marketing and design consultant. Trained in the United States. Experience mainly in fields of furniture, silverware, crystal, packaging and graphics. Head of Department of Design and Product Development, Semperit A. G Austria.

Belgium:

ANTOINE DE VINCK:
Industrial product designer, sculptor, potter. Recent work has been concerned with toys, glass, and lighting appliances. Particularly interested in natural history and ecology.

Bulgaria:

DMITRI PETROV:
Industrial designer.

Finland:

BORJE RAJALIN:
Runs own design office. Present work involves product, interior (mainly offices and stores) and exhibition design. During 1972–74 had research grant to investigate the design problems of small enterprises in the under-developed areas of Finland.

Great Britain:

RONALD FACIUS:
Consultant designer. At present concerned with visual education, especially the use of animated film to explain mathematical concepts. Previously worked in fields of packaging, exhibitions, engineering products and environmental cleaning.

Ireland:

MICHAEL BAMBER:
Architect. Works for Shannon Free Airport Development Company. Recent projects have included Celtic Museum and "Rent-an-Irish-Cottage" holiday homes.

FERGUS HOGAN:
Architect. Teaches at School of Architecture Dublin. In private practice has dealt with hotel and holiday village projects, housing, ships, office buildings and filling stations.

DAITHI HANLY:
Architect-planner. Now in private practice as consultant in architecture, town planning and landscape design. Formerly Dublin City Architect.

MARY KING:
Architect. Now works for Irish Tourist Board as interior designer, advising hotels and private people adapting their homes to provide tourist accommodation.

QUENTIN MITCHELL:
Staff designer Irish Television Studios.

DENIS ROBSON:
Architect. Works for National Monuments Branch. Office of Public Works, Dublin.

GUSTAV SAUTER:
Consultant interior architect and product designer. Particularly interested in design work for hotels.

JENNY TRIGWELL:
Textile designer. Now staff textile designer at Kilkenny Design Workshops. Previously worked for silk printers in London.

Israel:
ARTHUR GOLDREICH:
Architect. Head of Department of Environmental Design in University of Jerusalem. Professional work is primarily connected with hotels and public buildings.

Japan:
AKINOBU WATANABE:
Architect. Staff designer for the International Planning Department of GK Industrial Design Associates, Tokyo. Projects have included self-service restaurants, recreation centres, a ski-lodge, prefabricated houses and the IBM showroom in Tokyo.

Kenya:
LORNA SCHOFIELD:
Design student. Formerly nurse. Now working for design degree at the University of Nairobi.

USA:
HAIG KHACHATOORIAN:
Industrial and graphic designer. Trained in Poland and USA. Worked for Scope Exhibits, San Francisco and taught at City College. Has carried out product design and graphic work for a number of American industrial companies.

Yugoslavia:
GREGA KOSAK:
Freelance architect and designer. Projects include Yugoslav pavilion at Milan Triennale, seaside resort village, motel, snackbars.

MIRKO STOJNIC:
Architect and consultant designer—environment, interiors, furnishing. Projects have included road information systems, petrol stations, hotel interiors.